Wit,
Wisdom
& Moxie

Wit, Wisdom & Moxie

A Fundraiser's Compendium of
Wrinkles, Strategies, and Admonitions
That Really Work

Jerold Panas

Bonus Books, Inc
Chicago

OTHER BOOKS BY JEROLD PANAS

Finders Keepers: Lessons I've Learned about Dynamic Fundraising

Mega Gifts: Who Gives Them, Who Gets Them

Born to Raise: What Makes a Great Fundraiser; What Makes a Fundraiser Great

Boardroom Verities: A Celebration of Trusteeship with Some Guides and Techniques to Govern by

06   05   04   03   02   5   4   3   2   1

Library of Congress Control Number 2002101224

ISBN 1-56625-179-6

Bonus Books, Inc.
160 E. Illinois St.
Chicago, IL 60611

Printed in the United States of America

Table of Contents

This Is How It Began

I'll bet you've faced the same nagging problem I have. It drives me crazy. At least it used to. Now I've found a solution. I'll pass it along to you.

Here's what I'm talking about.

You get something very special in the mail you want to be certain to keep. Maybe it's a funny fundraising cartoon. Or an exciting brochure you'll want to read once more (or steal!). An article you want to save. Or some statistics you'll use someday for a speech, or quote at a board meeting to dazzle the directors.

But where do you file it? The piece doesn't fit any particular category. All of a sudden, you begin to identify with the song "Bewitched, Bothered, and

Bewildered!" You certainly don't want to throw it away—but there's no logical place to file it.

So you stick it in one of the piles on your desk. But in time that pile grows and keeps getting moved until it's at the edge of the desk. Or maybe you put it in a drawer (along with a sample marble paperweight someone wants you to buy for donors, phone calls you haven't returned, the nametag from last year's conference, and the "to-do" sheets from 1999 and 2000).

Well, I've come up with a solution that will astound you and make you forever grateful to me. Like all the great discoveries (electricity, the wheel, gravity—although I'm too modest to include mine with that group!), it's so simple you'll curse yourself for not thinking of it first.

Here's what I did. (I give praise and prayers to Saint Rita—that patron of impossible deeds.) Several years ago I started a file called **Good Stuff!** In it, I started putting all the bits and pieces I wanted to save—too good to throw away, but not sure where to file. The original *Good Stuff!* file has now grown into a pretty good-sized box.

Wit, Wisdom & Moxie

The other day, I showed my publisher some of the delicious morsels I've saved in my *Good Stuff!* box. He said he thought I might have something of interest to others in the fundraising world. So I dug into the box and chose some pieces I consider to be some of the best, the wisest, and the most fun.

In *Wit, Wisdom & Moxie*, I've included a sampling of some of these pieces. Everything here is material I've written—except where I've noted otherwise. I hope you enjoy the book. (Start your own *Good Stuff!* file and soon you'll have a book, too!)

Here's another tip. You know all of those personal notes you've wanted to keep? Maybe a letter of appreciation from a board member or an unexpected message that has special meaning, a photo of you with the chair of the Gala, a kind memo from the boss, a newspaper clipping about you— those sorts of things. I started a file called *Rainy Day* in which I put those special pieces. That file has grown into a box, too. I figure that some day, when I have time, I'm going to dig into my *Rainy Day* box and read all that stuff. What wonderful memories. (If you want to send me a complimentary letter, I'll be certain to add it to the box. Don't bother with a nasty note—I won't keep it!)

Wit,
Wisdom
& Moxie

The Joy of Being a Fundraiser

A fundraiser stood at the heavenly gate.
His face was scarred and old.
He stood before the man of fate
For admission to the fold.
"What have you done," Saint Peter said,
"To gain admission here?"
"I've been a fundraiser, sir," he said,
"For many and many a year."
The pearly gates swung open wide,
Saint Peter rang the bell.
"Come in and choose your harp," he sighed,
"You've had your share of hell!"

Your job, the very focus of what you must do, is to change a prospect's view of your institution from "they" and "them" to "we" and "us." When that happens, you'll have the financial and leadership commitments you require. You'll have the spiritual, moral, and dollar support you need. That's how easy it is.

The "doyen" of direct mail, **Mal Warwick**, reminded me again the other day about the power of a longer letter versus a short one. Longer copy pulls better. Period.

In a recent test, a four-pager received an 18 percent higher response than the shorter two-page letter. The total revenue was higher and the average gift was higher.

Adding the name of the signer of the letter to the outside upper left-hand corner of the envelope, along with a return address, increases the response to your mailing. It gets them into the package. You still have a challenge ahead, but you're well on your way.

A leader must be willing to take the risk, the blame, the brunt, and the storm. Never take the easy way. Never safety first. There is a zeal for adventure. A willingness to endure. A devotion to work. A passion to win.

My office called the chief officer in 20 different development offices. We got through to only three . . . and got 17 voicemails. No kidding—17! In the case of the 17, 12 advised that if we wanted to speak to their assistant, we were to dial another number. We tried the 12, and got voicemail eight times.

All organizations have donors—and prospects—who call. What's their reaction to voicemail? At CASE (Council for Advancement and Support of Education), there's a sign on the wall: Has anyone called CASE today and spoken to a real person?

Start a revolution: have someone in the office answer the phone.

Your institution doesn't have needs. People have needs. People have problems and concerns. Your institution has the response, the solution. **Sell the response, not the need.**

*T*rue North must be the compass of every path you take, the guiding star of your life and fate. Soaring standards, steadfast character, uncompromising integrity—these provide the True North to life's compass.

Wayne Herron gives a lesson from which we can all learn. Wayne, development officer at Pasadena's Fuller Theological Seminary, started to acknowledge personally all gifts of $100 and above—with a phone call and a personal handwritten note.

He called one regular $200 donor—an older man with no obvious net worth. He didn't come up on the radar in any of those dollar-sweeps of the database. He didn't show up anywhere as having even a minimum net worth. But Wayne called him anyway. They spoke for about an hour.

A waste of time? Hardly!

Herron learned a lot about the man's life, his work, family, and church. Herron probed and asked questions. The man said he would like to set up a small annuity, tying it to a program in one of Fuller's schools. Three weeks later the $200-giver set up a six-figure annuity. There will be more to come.

The lesson: don't take anyone for granted. People want to be recognized, acknowledged, and thanked. A telephone call opened the way for the gift. There are many such diamonds waiting to be mined for your organization.

*D*o it now. *Wavering and vacillation lead to the street of by-and-by that reaches the house of never.*

In our seminars and our work with clients, I've stopped teaching how to "Ask for the Gift." I know better now. But it has taken me time to learn the lesson.

Here's how simple it is: The more you know about the donor, the more you get the donor to speak, and the more you listen . . . the more effective you are in having the donor tell you the size of the gift and what he or she wants to give to.

So now I'm preaching, "Listen the Gift." It means that in a solicitation situation, you speak 25 percent of the time and you listen 75 percent of the time. It works. It really does.

You have two ears and one mouth. That should tell you something about the importance of listening.

Great trustees don't just happen. They are selectively recruited, carefully oriented, vigorously encouraged, and inspired to greatness. You don't elect trustees—you pick them.

What counts is not just what we are against, but what we are for. Who leads us is less important than what leads us. Convictions, courage, faith—these are the signposts that pilot us to a life of integrity.

"There's bad news, good news, and bad news."

That's how the chair began his remarks at the kick-off of one of our recent campaigns. "The bad news is that we sorely need a new science building. The good news is that we do have the money for it. The bad news is that it is still in your pockets!"

The group responded with applause . . . and spontaneous pledges of $11 million at the meeting in individual gifts. And that's *really* good news!

Public opinion research is scarce on attitudes towards telemarketing. The overriding perception is that people do not like to be called for a gift.

In the state of Vermont last year, a public opinion poll was conducted. It gave overwhelming substantiation that most people (over 85 percent) object to receiving telemarketing calls at home. It's even worse when they get calls at the office.

*D*on't put it off. *Let procrastination be considered your personal treason and treachery. Regard delay, dawdling, and dalliance repugnant to soul and spirit.*

It's one of the truisms of our business—a dramatic and compelling case statement with a sense of urgency sets the stage for a successful ask. But wait. There's a problem. The same case statement doesn't touch every constituency in the same way.

Take a hospital, for example. Physicians have a much different reason for giving than a grateful patient. And employees different than major donors. In a university, the faculty has a different rationale for giving than alumni.

Try testing different case statements for specific constituencies. You'll see how effective it is. Develop creatively conceived case statements . . . skewed at important points to the distinct group you're trying to reach.

Ask your trustees to host cultivation events in their homes . . . from intimate dinner to large cocktail parties. These events can be significant for your development program . . . but a major added bonus is the satisfaction trustees receive when they do something important for the institution.

The world seeks those who are willing to throw themselves into the battle. Who take a position unconventional. Who give heart and spirit to the terror, the surprise, the fear, and the exhilaration of the unexplored.

I'm finding that there is much less tendency today towards reciprocal gifts. ("I'll give to your favorite charity if you'll give to mine.") The concept of obligation or paying back a favor may land a small gift, but don't count on a major gift because of a *quid pro quo*. Most tell us that when it comes to making a major gift, they give to institutions they are engaged in and whose mission they are committed to. If there isn't a deep interest in the program, they are willing to say *no* to a friend or to one who has given to them for their cause.

Some CEOs and board members expect immediate fundraising results. But it takes time to put a strong development program into place. Everyone needs to understand that.

Si Seymour, author of the best-selling *Designs for Fund Raising*, said: "If you want alfalfa, you can raise several crops a year. But if you want oats, it will take little longer." Tell your leaders to be prepared to make the investment required for the type of gifts you seek—those at the highest level possible. Just make certain that you have a plan in place which is time-phased and detailed, and that you are working it. Plan the work, work the plan.

*T*hese fleeting, runaway opportunities will never again be captured.
Pledge now, right now, to the commitment of TNT: **Today, Not Tomorrow**.
That's the essence of a rewarding and fulfilling life—TNT.

Ken **Walker**, one of our writers, prepares his case statements in an unusual way. He writes the opening page that sparks the reader's interest and sympathy, and touches the institution's pulse . . . and then writes the final page, "solemnizing the marriage of potential and opportunity, the grand closure, the summation that elicits an energetic agreement based on specific realities and the highest assured principles."

Walker says that some case statements lie on the page without a quiver, while others grab the reader and don't let go. He obviously delivers the latter.

Women are more effective . . . but you knew this all along! If your organization does telemarketing, be certain to use females to call other women. You'll find that they are much more successful in getting the gift.

*B*elieve it or not, over the years I have discovered these in various church bulletins:

1. *This afternoon there will be a meeting in the south and north ends of the church. Children will be baptized at both ends.*

2. *Thursday at 5 P.M. there will be a meeting of the Little Mothers Club. All ladies wishing to be Little Mothers please meet with Pastor in his study.*

3. *This being Easter Sunday, we will ask Mrs. Johnson to come forward and lay an egg at the altar.*

4. *The ladies of the church have cast off clothing of every kind and they may be seen in the church basement on Friday afternoon.*

5. *The rosebud on the altar this morning is to announce the birth of David Alan Belzer, the sin of Rev. and Mrs. Julius Belzer.*

The CEO and the board should annually review the institution's foremost strategic challenges. Set aside enough time that this can be done carefully, thoughtfully, and effectively.

The board's job is to assess the CEO's list to determine whether the challenges and opportunities have been accurately targeted and the issues properly developed and crafted. This can be a defining moment for the institution for it is here that the board and the CEO together make the future happen. There must be a fusion, total agreement, on the institution's priorities and strategic direction.

Becoming too friendly with a prospect can be a problem. It can get in the way of an effective solicitation. For some, close personal attachments block a strong solicitation. **Si Seymour** says, "A party is just a party to a volunteer. But a party is a business meeting to the professional fundraiser."

Be clear about your goal. Your objective is not to become a personal friend of the prospect, although that might happen. Your purpose is to win the respect and confidence of those you are courting.

*T*he time finally comes when every organization must plan or perish. It can be an agonizing moment.

New School University just completed a successful campaign for $200 million. What was special about that campaign is that it was the first in the history of this extraordinary institution—a "conglomerate" of seven quite diverse colleges. The university did not have a history of fundraising of any significance, nor did any of its colleges.

But that's not what is most remarkable about its campaign. What makes it singularly noteworthy is that 45 percent of the goal was given by its board. Let that be a lesson to you, one that you already knew: the board leads the way. We call it campaigning "from the inside, out."

John Tishman is chair and CEO of billion-dollar Tishman Realty & Construction, and chair of the university. He tells us that, "having a successful campaign like this is easy. All that is necessary is to have right board."

It can add special zest to a meeting to have the chair give others a turn at running the session. It's good for practice . . . and those who learn to lead, learn how to participate.

*I*n an organization, the beacon of integrity must burn with brilliance—because it lights the way for all activities and actions.

The David and Lucille Packard Foundation now has assets of $9.1 billion. It's among the largest foundations in the country. Soon after the death of David Packard, the board decided to develop a set of values and principles, five in all, to guide its future.

One that won't surprise you is their belief in individual leadership. "In grantmaking," they say, "our board and staff will look for those individuals and their nonprofit organizations best able to make a contribution in their fields and then will respect and support the board, their leadership and ideas." They are seeking the very best in staff leadership . . . and are willing to support it.

There's a growing trend for trustees to take on a greater responsibility in their giving. Last year, for instance, at private doctorate-granting institutions, the average gift from a board member was $78,000. At liberal arts colleges across the country, donations from board members have doubled in the past five years—up this past year to $17,000 per board member.

*T*o do something, no matter how small, to make others happier and better—this is the highest of all ambition, the most elevating hope, which can inspire a man or a woman.

Tell them how you used the money! **Richardson Love, Jr.,** is director of the Education Division for the Knight Foundation (Miami, Florida). He tells me that it's surprising how many recipients do not let the foundation know what happened as a result of its grant. Foundations (and individuals, also) want to know about the organization and those served by it.

Even if the results were not everything hoped for, it's important that you do a good job of reporting back. Unexpected or undesirable results do not necessarily mean a failure. Not every experiment produces a positive result. But the failures, the surprises, the unexpected, very often end up with meaningful outcomes.

Keep your donors informed. Every contact is a major step towards the next transaction.

I'm finding that more and more prospects are bringing up the topic of planned giving. There's a greater awareness of the concept than we have ever known before. Now's the time to really capitalize on this important aspect of your fundraising.

*T*wo wonderful phrases comprise the most glorious duet: "Will you help?" and "Yes, I will!"

If you're having trouble recruiting volunteers, you're not alone. There's been a decline nationally of 3 percent a year, each year for the past three years.

Yet, Americans believe keenly in volunteerism. Recent studies make this quite clear. Major reasons for the decline: 1) working mothers and fathers have less time to be away from home. 2) A perception that charities are not as ethical or honest as they once were. But the major reason is: **3) They were not asked!**

Virtually all who get involved feel they are playing a major role in making their communities and organizations better places. They feel their work is important. The same number feel that the organization does not communicate with them very well about how important their volunteerism is.

If giving from the board is not 100 percent, that's unacceptable . . . but the amount they give is also important. In your financial statements, where you list gifts, include a separate line for board members. This puts the spotlight where it belongs.

Philanthropy is the rent we pay for the joy and privilege we have for our space on this earth.

Gordon Pattee is a giver of note and a dedicated member of those boards he serves. As president of one board and chair of the nominating committee of another, he tells me he is quite clear with all members he recruits—they are expected to give $25,000 a year. He's not very tolerant of those who don't comply. He says, "It's easy. If they don't give, I ask them to leave the board."

What's interesting is that it seems the higher he raises the bar, the more people want to join. It puts the right folks in the right circle, he says.

What about those who can't afford $25,000, but contribute in other ways—service, work, wisdom? Pattee says, "Find another spot for them. They're too valuable to lose, but not necessarily the people you want on your board."

The level for your institution may not be $25,000. But what is important is that you set some level and start enlisting those who can make a difference. It's your future.

*T*hese are indeed great times, difficult times, complex times, for your
institution. But there have never
been more opportunities. And there has never
been a more exciting time to be a volunteer
for a great cause.

Dare to think big.

I heard this from an organization's loyal donor who complained, "I'm tired of you asking for nickels and dimes to keep this program running. What do you need to make it a big success?" The fundraiser told her and she responded with a $2 million gift.

Be audacious! I dare you to act bolder, more creatively . . . with unending dedication and determination. I dare you to get out of the box. I dare you . . . to seek new horizons and break through every barrier that keeps you from being the very best you can be.

Nothing can match a good letter that packs a compelling, emotionally appealing message—along with a sense of urgency. But the key is—a *really* good letter. That takes savvy and winning experience. That's best left to those who have expertise in the field.

A leader understands that the difference between failure and success is often the difference in doing something nearly right and doing it exactly right.

Be prepared for this scenario. The largest donor to one of our clients walked into the development office and demanded to see his files. Not the donor data-info kept on the computer, not that stuff. He wanted to see his files, clippings, call reports. He had heard that the office kept files on major donors.

His file happened to contain very specific information about his drinking problem and a messy divorce. His only comment when he left abruptly: "Well, you folks certainly keep extensive records."

By law, donors have a right to access their files. Think about it now and draft a policy as to how and where to keep sensitive information.

In a recent study among men and women 70 years of age and older, 87 percent said they would be willing to volunteer their time—if asked. Of the group, 63 percent had never been asked by any organization. You may be overlooking a gold mine of volunteer hours, commitment, and passion for your program.

They're waiting to be asked. Ask!

Wit, Wisdom & Moxie

When we come into this life, we don't really own anything. And we own nothing when we leave. It is only a lease we have during our lifetime—and it is up to us to make the most of it. When you leave this life, you want to be able to say: "I was given a certain talent—and I used it all."

1 In direct mail, target marketing and proper segmentation is essential—because it allows you to meet the prospects at their thinking and giving level. It lets you speak their language, know where they are in life, and understand their greatest motivations.

2 Make your mailings as personal as possible. For instance, refer to last year's gift. If possible, talk about the prospect's days on the football team or in the marching band. Or if the prospect was a patient, refer to the physician who took care of him or her. In every solicitation, tell how much you know about the prospect. It binds him or her to the institution.

3 Don't segment because you've read somewhere that segmentation is the thing to do. You must have distinctive and specific solicitation strategies, one for each of your separate constituencies. Make segmentation work for you. Have a plan, and then work at it.

4 Evaluate your database. Give highest priority to your previous donors and to high-potential donors. Those who have not done anything in the past, or those whose giving has lapsed for some years, are important—but don't spend as much time on them as you do on your priority list.

5 Your database is like a septic tank. (Does that comparison bother you?) If it's working well, you barely give it much thought. But nobody likes getting into a septic tank. If your database is not well maintained, you're going to have a real mess on your hands. Keep it in working order.

6 It's important to have as perfect a database as possible. But having immediate and easy access to it is the real key. If you're not able to select the constituencies you want quickly and with complete confidence, you won't be successful. You simply won't do well in the highly competitive world of direct marketing.

7 You're certain you've done everything right. You've had an expert develop the package and write the copy. You've segmented the various audiences in an effective way. The copy was directed to each particular group. But . . . the mailing was a dismal failure. Don't despair. It doesn't always work, no matter how effective the strategy or the package. Don't be discouraged—try new approaches and make certain that your boss understands that not every mailing will be a roaring success. (Better make certain the boss knows that in advance.)

8 Oh . . . and one thing more. I really believe in segmentation, but too many segments will drive you crazy. It will be counterproductive, will cause stress and strain, and will likely be hazardous to your emotional well being!

Keep in touch with your major donors. In a study I just completed, a potential seven-figure donor spoke highly of the institution's work and mission. But he said he actually knew little about the organization. He asked who the executive director was and how long he had been in the job. When I told him he'd been there seven years, he said, "I know this sounds immodest, but I am one of the leaders in the community. Doesn't it surprise you that the executive director wouldn't even take time to come by and say hello, not in seven years?"

Despite the prospect's interest in the organization and its mission . . . it won't get the gift it should. Not until some executive attention is paid.

Here's a great way to personalize your phonathon. When you send the acknowledgement and pledge arrangement—include a photo of the caller holding a large card that says: "Thank you." On the back of the photo, have the caller write a few words of appreciation.

*I*t is hard to outdo the Lord in generosity.

Tests emphatically demonstrate that citing the problems and challenges your organization faces is far less effective than talking about your opportunities, results, and successes.

That's true of both direct-mail and one-on-one solicitations.

Donors want to hear the good news, positive outcomes, and results that count. That's what will keep them giving. Don't talk about your needs. Stress your results.

Count on it: The cost of direct mail will continue to rise. Higher postage, that's certain. Higher cost of production and handling.

Begin thinking now about alternative methods for securing new donors and renewing old friends.

If you're not planning on e-donations and Electronic Fund Transfer, you're already losing your place in the parade.

Words and dreams are over-abundant. But ideas that rouse can change the world. A person touches the highest pinnacle of fulfillment when he or she is consumed in the quest of an idea.

Life membership is a flawed concept. In a development department assessment of a medical center, I noted 186 "Life Members." Not bad! Well . . . on further examination—not good at all!

The Life Member category was started eight years ago—for a gift of $10,000. I found that only 23 in this group have made a gift since their original $10,000.

I strongly advise against the idea of life membership. If you already have this category, and you suffer the same dilemma most do . . . I recommend eliminating it. Get rid of it. For all those who are currently Lifers . . . give them plenty of recognition, throw a party, put their names on a plaque, whatever. You don't want them to get angry . . . but you don't want to perpetuate the group.

You want friends who continue to give for life, and beyond. The problem with life membership is that, too often, it's a way of getting out of giving.

*I*t is much better to give than to receive—and it's deductible!

L ess is more.

I'm finding increasing donor disenchantment with fancy, embossed, four-color brochures. **Chris Hellman** (chair and major benefactor, San Francisco Ballet) says she and her friends like to give—but don't like expensive brochures. "It's a turn-off."

Study your situation carefully. Determine if something less slick, less ostentatious, can do the job. Eschew the award. Go for the gift!

For most of our major-gift, high-end prospects, I like to use a 3-ring binder with plain photocopying and photos. At the Chicago Botanic Garden, where they're on their way to a successful $10 million endowment campaign, the major-gift material is 3-ring bound and produced at a photocopying store. Best of all—no one has ever thrown away a three-ring binder!

I find, by the way, that videos pack great punch. And isn't it interesting—I haven't heard anyone say, "That must have been an expensive video!"

*T*he difference between winning and losing, between being the best and being near-best, is practice. Practice and hard work. Practice doesn't make perfect. Perfect practice makes perfect. And that means work. Hard work.

Alan **Shawn Feinstein** has given more than $50 million to a center that feeds the hungry. He says he would not have given the money—he didn't even know the organization. But a social worker from a community center in Providence, Rhode Island, called and asked him to visit the center.

He went for a visit. He saw the lines of hungry people, the crushing poverty. He couldn't get it out of his mind. "I never knew there was such an overt hunger in Rhode Island," he says. "No one ever talked about it. When I saw it, I knew I had to help."

It started with someone urging him to visit the center. Don't just sit passively waiting for donors to come to you. Reach out, make the call. Get them to see what you're doing!

Here's a simple answer: when asked by a donor how much he or she should give, the best reply will be: **"Give until you are proud."**

Y ou hear it all the time: the clatter and clang of those trembling and trepid souls who regularly remind you, "It can't be done!" and, "We've never done it that way!" But you know this to be true—that no great plan is accomplished without overcoming endless obstacles which test the mettle of your determination and the endurance of your faith.

In a very quick, unscientific review of the Web sites of a variety of organizations (hospitals and medical centers, colleges and universities, YMCAs, Red Cross, and so forth)—three out of four do not include any information, or information that is virtually impossible to determine— about their development effort, or why philanthropy is important to the organization, or how to make a gift. And that includes some of our own clients. Correct it now!

If you have a Web site—and, of course, you all should—be certain you make it easy and convenient for viewers to make a gift to your great cause.

Find out *why* you didn't get the gift.

If a foundation has turned you down, discover the reason. Most foundations are quite willing to share their rationale. They will take the time to explain why you missed the mark.

And guess what! It sets the stage for your next proposal.

It's absolutely amazing what you don't get when you don't ask.

Leaders are born—and made. That's what Korn/Ferry, one of the world's preeminent search firms, says about leadership. Qualities such as charisma, temperament, and presence are inherent. But many characteristics can be learned.

The study indicates that a powerful, inspiring all-encompassing vision is the attribute that most characterizes the leader and empowers the organization—a vision that can motivate everyone to achieve goals previously thought impossible. The leader makes the staff and the volunteers reach mountaintops they never though they would be able to climb.

If someone accepts the privilege of serving on a board, the responsibility to serve it well is implicit. If the organization is not one of their number one or two priorities for time, interest, and money, they should probably move on to a different organization. What you need are board members with passion for the organization, who will give and work to their full capacity.

Momentum is a critical quality for success. It is the force that electrifies an institution and ignites the spirit. It assures growth and vitality. It forges through the past to barrier-breaking opportunities. It moves mission into motion.

In an organization, momentum makes all things possible. It converts individuals into a team of dogged devotion and resolve. It propels men and women beyond personal horizons and unites them in a common cause.

An organization with momentum has an impelling and infectious urge and surge. A rolling, roaring, raging determination and drive. An undisciplined fervor for the fray and fire.

You can strengthen the giving of the board . . . but be careful, you might lose some trustees. Here's how to do it right. Show both the aggregate and the annual giving of all directors. Show their giving as a separate line-item on your financial statement.

Have the Chair and a small committee decide whether this is appropriate for your organization. We feel it is. Most foundation and corporate grantors are asking for this information to accompany proposals. Why shouldn't the board be allowed to see it for themselves?

If you are squeamish at all about embarrassing those who give time but not money, figure out what value you place on their time, calculate the hours or days, and compute that.

Success is a matter of luck. Ask any failure.

It pays to advertise.

If you're looking for volunteers, try the classified section of your local newspaper. It will open up a whole new world beyond your known constituency.

Several years ago, one of my clients (a Salvation Army) found notable success with a classified ad. They received 46 responses. After some interviewing, they found that 19 were really interested in the program and would be able to make successful and fulfilling contributions as volunteers. A year later, 15 of the group were still in place.

According to a study just completed by **Kittleman and Associates**, a major executive search firm, the number one cause of stress for fundraisers is having too much to do and too little time. That doesn't surprise me!

*I*f you find a path with no obstacles, it probably doesn't lead anywhere.

Look. Hook. Book.

These are three basics of a good direct-mail piece.

The package must have a special **look** to it. It has got to stand out. There has got to be an irresistible **hook**, a tug that a prospect simply can't avoid. And finally, the **book**—stories about how your organization provides life-changing answers to real people with real problems.

Donald Kirk, who heads the Union Gospel Mission in Sacramento, tells me about a recent confrontation within his board. The members disagreed on whether they should accept a large gift from a donor who some of the board felt represented "tainted money." Don made a plea to take the funds because they could be put to such great use among the homeless and those in need, and finished his remarks by saying: "If we don't have the money, *'t'ain't* going to be here to use." They accepted the gift!

Wit, Wisdom & Moxie

A genius is someone who shoots at a target no one else ever sees—and hits it.

Put your copy to the acid test.

Packages like Microsoft Word have ways to test the grade level of your copy. In Word, it's a selection called "grammar" under the "tools" menu.

If you want your mail to be quickly understood, read, and absorbed—write at an eighth grade level. Don't for a moment think that it's "writing down."

Write short paragraphs, two or three sentences at the most. And write short sentences. No more than six or eight words.

There's more.

Try paragraphs with just one or two words. They will be read. Use words of two syllables, three at the most.

Practice this in your correspondence, direct mail, and printed material. It will be read.

*V*olunteering is a priceless commodity. It's the only thing you can give away and still keep for your own.

"People give to people" is as old a fundraising saw as exists. The trouble is that it isn't really true.

People don't give to people. They give to causes and missions they believe in, they give to programs and organizations they are involved in.

The solicitor with a great deal of leverage can make the appointment or help open the door— and the donor may end up making a small gift, a token out of friendship. But that won't get the major gift.

It is a very special and precious bonus if you have leadership that has access to a prospect. That's an important beginning. You will have an opportunity to present your vision and dreams. But if the prospect doesn't believe in the institution, and better still have some direct involvement in its program, you will not receive a major gift.

Wit, Wisdom & Moxie

I *am sometimes asked about the spiritual, or Biblical, roots of philanthropy. There are countless references. I particularly like St. Paul's second letter to the people of Corinth.Writing about the churches of Macedonia, he reports:*

"During a severe ordeal of affliction, their abundant joy and their extreme poverty have overflowed in a wealth of generosity on their part . . . they voluntarily gave according to their means, and even beyond their means . . .

"So we want you to excel also in this generous undertaking. I do not say this as a command, but I am testing the genuineness of your love against the earnestness of others . . . I do not mean that there should be relief for others and pressure on you, but it is a question of fair balance between your present and their relief."

Be unrelenting in telling your story. Hammer away at it. Tell about the lives you have saved today, the lives you have changed and enriched.

Organize and structure your plan for reaching your top prospects and donors. Let them know what makes you different than any other organization doing similar work. Dramatize your uniqueness. Don't miss a single opportunity. Put your plan in writing.

Focus on the interest of your donors, not the needs of your organization. Remember: You don't have needs, people have needs.

On a regular basis, we review whether it is better to have gifts and memberships renewable throughout the year on a monthly basis . . . or all come due at the same time of the year. We almost always opt for the former. It spreads your revenue throughout the year instead of putting your budget in jeopardy if some unforeseen situation arises when all gifts and memberships become renewable. It also allows you to concentrate your efforts on renewals year-round.

*R*isks are not to be avoided. They are to be relished! The untried and the unknown are challenges and opportunities to be met head-on.

Show proper appreciation to those who have made estate plans and planned gifts. Make them proud.

Most organizations have a special "society" or group that recognizes estate notes and planned gifts. If you don't have one, you should.

You can guarantee that the group will grow in size if you give recognition. List the names in every publication that goes out, in your monthlies and quarterlies. List the names in your annual report. List them on a wall. Shout it from the rooftops. Have a small committee work on how you can even give added recognition. These dear friends need to know that you will never forget them.

Success in the past is no assurance of success in the future. Over one-third of the firms in the Fortune 500 fifteen years ago no longer exist. In today's world, you have to run very fast to stay in place. Survival, growth, and greater market share depend on your financial vitality and the strength and commitment of your board.

R eputation is what others think of you. Your true character is what God and the angels know of you. All of your actions and expressions will be as simple as the truth.

It's okay to use an outsider to write your mission statement. In fact, it's a good idea.

Why not? You use an outsider to design your logo and brochures, and an outsider to write your case statement. Why not use someone particularly effective to write the most consequential statement of the institution?

Try this. Even if you have a mission statement which you feel is relevant and working for you, have a meeting with a small group—trustees, a staff person or two, and someone served by the institution. Have a writer present. Have the group talk about what the organization is all about, what its dreams are, and what you hope to achieve in the lives of people. Have the writer take copious notes and put it all into a new statement. Compare the old and the new.

Blessings overflow and are unceasing. Be thankful for robust health to make life and work a joy. Wealth enough to support your needs and those in need. And determination to make each day better than the day before. Boundless happiness to share with others. Strength and spirit unbridled to overcome all obstacles. And unremitting optimism to vanish all doubts. Grace to overcome and forgive any transgressions. Patience to remain calm while the world races by. Love enough to conquer all. And a caring outstretched hand, especially to young people. To know that in the central place of every heart must be respect for the earth, peace for the people, delight in the good, forgiveness for past wrongs, and passion for new beginnings. And above all, abiding thanks for all our gains, miracle after miracle. To know that our final victories come from hope and faith and love and gratitude. Unleash the power within you so you can touch the lives of others in endless and wondrous ways. Make every day a hallowed day of thanksgiving.

Your mission statement should be in words that even a sixth grader can understand. If you fail this test, start all over.

Don't use the word "quality"—that should be a given.

Keep it short. Two sentences, perhaps three. No more.

It should be memorable. Good enough that it can be easily memorized. It should be packed with energy, zeal, and commitment.

And finally, it must vividly describe your institution's uniqueness. If it doesn't make clear how you are distinct, offering services in a way unlike any other organization—it makes you a me-too, carbon-copy organization.

Our studies show that when you do your telemarketing in-house instead of outsourcing it, the number of contacts improves, the number of dollars is about the same, and your collections improve markedly.

Wit, Wisdom & Moxie

Courage requires ambition, audacity, and an unflagging will to succeed. It demands a drive to be different. It means scraping and escaping the barnacles of old ideas. A driving determination to plunge, to speculate, to inquire, to imagine, to explore.

Wit, Wisdom & Moxie

MY IRREFUTABLE LAWS OF FUNDRAISING

The Law of Setting the Campaign Goal
Accuracy is a crutch for those who can't cope with fantasy

The Law of Analysis Paralysis
I haven't made the call yet because I need more research

The Law of Aiming Too High on an Ask
Jumping a chasm in two leaps

The Law of Calling on a Key Prospect
If you dance with a gorilla, the gorilla leads

The Law of Getting the Gift
If you think you can—you're right
If you think you can't—you're right

The Law of Frivolity
Time spent on any item of a board agenda will be in inverse proportion to its importance to the future of the organization.

The Law of Over-selling to Get a Gift
The more you run over a dead cat, the flatter it gets

The Law of Handling a Difficult Call
No matter which way you spit, it's upwind

The Law of Waiting for Precisely the Right Time to Ask

Ready, Aim, Aim, Aim, Aim, Aim!

The Law of Working with a Tough Campaign Chair

When you starve with a tiger, the tiger starves last

The Law of Campaign Common Sense

If you and two friends are chased by a grizzly bear, you don't have to run faster than the grizzly bear—you just have to run faster than your two friends

The Law of Maintaining the Campaign Calendar

The fast, slippery track is lined with banana peels and fired campaign directors

The Law of the Professional Fundraising Consultant

To do good is noble. To give advice and counsel to those who do good is also noble—and much less trouble

More and more of our clients are going to a performance-based compensation system. In the past, most attention was focused on past performance, rather than specific goals for the future.

The objectives can be based on amount raised, gift and membership renewals, amount of media attention generated, number of contacts and calls, effectiveness of stewardship, number of committees that are staffed, and so forth. If the incentive is based on a fixed amount, rather than a percentage, it does not violate the code of ethics.

Opponents feel that donors may not feel comfortable with this type of an arrangement, but what profession (attorneys, surgeons) and which corporations (IBM, Xerox) don't use an incentive?

One of the greatest benefits is that the board and staff need to work together in developing guidelines and a strategic structure.

Consider an incentive program for your organization. See if it makes sense for you.

*S*uccess in life is determined by the character of your journey. It is your testament to impeccable and rigid standards, an unwillingness to settle for anything less than enduring and unshakable principles. Your life and integrity are inseparable. It is your blood and flesh.

How many ways can you thank a donor? Not enough.

One of the national campaigns I'm working with is naming a revered elder statesman of the organization to be in charge just of donor stewardship—just to be sure that the donor is never forgotten, never taken for granted.

He will do this in many ways, including one of the most effective that is too little used—a simple phone call. The call can happen immediately. There's no waiting for a receipt, a letter, or a signature—though of course this should follow.

I got a call like that recently from an organization to which I had made a gift. I kept waiting for the caller to get to the point, then finally caught on that he had made his point. He was just calling to say thanks.

That felt good.

The one who never walks except where there are tracks will never make any discoveries.

People give to you because there is no other organization that performs quite the service you do in the very special way you do it. You are uniquely positioned to perform your services. Men and women want to give to you because of the extraordinary way you change lives and save lives.

In order to give dramatic clarity and emotional definition to your mission, have a half-day session with some of your key people. I like doing this in two separate groups—one with staff and the other with board members (with staff present as facilitators). You can have large groups, but keep the discussion units small—six to nine people.

Talk about what makes you different, why you are stand-outs in your field, what you do that no one else is doing, and how you do it better than anyone else.

Is it worth the time? You bet.

Take good notes. Enlist a committee that will be responsible for implementation—how you begin integrating this useful information into service and public relations.

Wit, Wisdom & Moxie

*M*en and women of talent—willing to sacrifice and work—make the discoveries, write the books, produce the arts, win the campaigns, and order the world. New actions. New aspirations. New efforts. New vision. All these are due less to genius than to perseverance and determination.

Philanthropy isn't optional, that's what **Anita Roddick** says. She's the founder of the very successful Body Shop.

She tells me that when a philanthropist responds to community needs, he or she is investing in the future of the community. "So philanthropy is as much an act of faith as it is an expression of optimism. More than just goodness or generosity, it is simply what you have to do."

It continues to be a difficult time financially for healthcare institutions, and it's likely to get worse before it gets better. I like the approach of Florida Hospital (Orlando) in one of their appeals: "That doesn't mean we're not good enough to earn a profit. What it means is that rather than paying our profit out to shareholders, our profit is reinvested into the community."

It's hard to argue with that kind of logic and warmth.

A loser says, "I can't do it." A winner says, "I can't do it **yet**."

It's not your fancy four-color brochure, and it's not your case statement. The most effective piece in your campaign tool chest is a **"Question & Answer"** folder. And it need not be fancy at all.

My experience with campaign Q&As is that they are an effective way to supplement the case. And our research shows that they are by far the best-read material of anything you do. The format somehow invites readership.

It's easy. Choose the fifteen or so questions that will be most often asked about your project . . . and then hone the list to eight. If there are more than eight truly biting issues, your campaign is likely in trouble! Make the response to the questions simple and direct. Don't waffle.

Sometimes Q&As are prepared for volunteers—and those may have questions about different methods of giving. But I'm not an advocate of using those kinds of questions in the piece that goes to prospects.

*W*atch out for phony fundraising solutions. When you spot a quack, duck.

Choosing the title for a campaign or a case statement can be tough. Here are some good rules to follow. Limit the title to very few words, three or four at most—and those words should flow easily and poetically. It should capture, or at least touch, the heart and purpose of the institution. And finally, it should not have been seen or used recently. A good rule to follow is to eschew the word "excellence"!

Planned giving grows . . . and gets younger.

The number who included charity in their wills increased from 5.7 percent in 1992 to eight percent today—40 percent growth. But here's the big news that may surprise you. You've been thinking your greatest potential is with those in their 60s or 70s, but I'm finding now that the average age when the first charitable bequests are made is 49 and the first will is written at 44.

Take another look at who you're targeting and who is receiving your material.

*I*t's the start that stops most people.

The most important contribution a CEO can make to the institution's development effort is to articulate his or her vision of the institution persistently, persuasively, and passionately. And to do so with such urgency and drama that it is shared by all constituents. And to do so with such convincing inspiration that all feel it is indeed their own vision and dream.

In *Quantum Leap Thinking*, **James J. Mabes** says: "It is a common misunderstanding to equate a mission statement with a vision—a mission statement comes from the head, a vision comes from the heart. Vision is creating an ideal future with a grand purpose . . . vision is about greatness." This book is a must-read (Dove Books, Beverly Hills, California).

Here's an important distinction to keep in mind. The annual gift is almost always to meet the needs of the institution. The major gift is always to meet the needs in the life of a donor. Keep that in mind when framing your strategy for the call. You'll get the gift.

We are all faced with great opportunities . . . brilliantly disguised as impossible situations.

In a study conducted recently for the Denver Foundation, it was found that among those who give to charity, 61 percent also indicate that they volunteer. The more they volunteer and are involved, the more they give. These figures won't surprise any of you but it confirms that you need to get key people involved. And once you do, the gifts will follow.

The same study also shows that those who reported their religion as being "very important" donated more than those who rated it less important.

To resign . . . or be fired? Let's hope it doesn't happen to you, but if it does, and you're given the option—which do you choose?

We find that it doesn't really matter. Both require some explanation and "resignation" sends out a warning signal to a prospective employer.

Wit, Wisdom & Moxie

We live in a time of unparalleled dynamism. In today's world, when something has been done a particular way for two years or so, it is a pretty good sign that it is being done the wrong way.

You're falling behind if you don't have e-mail addresses for at least 30 percent of your database. Aim for 50 percent.

Develop a strategy now for seeking e-mail addresses from prospects, members, and donors. Have a plan and implement it.

We recently collected return envelopes from 23 organizations. Only one asked for an e-mail address—although the others requested all the other typical information.

The parade will pass you by. Put a plan in place now.

Incentive pay pays! The University of California, Irvine, is using an incentive plan that augments a pay-for-performance for major gift fundraisers. Fundraising totals have increased almost 100 percent.

What about the ethics? You'd better discuss and settle that with your top volunteers. But they will be impressed. UCI is achieving a fifteen percent better return on its investment in fundraising.

Wit, Wisdom & Moxie

*I*n our profession, you learn to take rejection in stride . . . you understand that a series of NOs only means that you are part way toward a YES.

Keep a professional journal. At the end of each working day, take ten minutes to summarize your activities and accomplishments. Visits, calls, special contacts. Indicate the result and what follow-up actions are required.

The suggestion comes from **Paul Schneiter**, editor and publisher of *Planned Gifts Counselor*.

He says that in his dozen years as a professional, he referred to his journal constantly. It saved him untold grief. One time, it helped to close a significant gift from a board member who had "forgotten" about a pledge he made in a trustee meeting. When he saw the entry in Paul's journal, he suddenly "remembered" and completed the gift.

Try it. Give it six months. We think you'll find it invaluable.

In the past few years, there has been a significant trend for CEOs to change their title from "executive director" to "president/ CEO." In many cases, the CEO now has a vote on board.

There is a nobility about hard work. Even the weariness it leaves is exhilarating. Hard work is not hard work at all to the enthusiast. It is intoxicating. The privations. The hardships. The long days and long nights. All are worth the price, and the price is always worth it— results and success.

I find that the Clorox Company (Oakland, California) is about as inventive and encouraging regarding volunteerism as any corporation I know. But now, I see this attitude more and more among enlightened corporations.

At Clorox, all junior and senior officers are encouraged to serve on boards, particularly where Clorox has the greatest interest.

There is CEO support for each officer to serve on at least one nonprofit board. And the company foundation backs that up with funding.

Writing a mission statement is a valuable experience. It forces you to think and describe why you really exist. But some statements are obtuse. I was at a board meeting the other day at which one person, peeling away the layers of rhetoric that covered up the core purpose of the organization, finally concluded that the real mission was: "to survive."

*T*he innovative organization has the power to connect the seemingly unconnected. To perceive what others have not seen, and to create what no one else has thought to attempt. To dare what others were too timid to try.

It does not ask, "Can we do this?" but rather, "**How** can we do it?" It recognizes that to say "impossible" always puts it on the losing side.

If you want to develop a direct-mail package that will work for you, one of the most effective ways is to save all of the packages you receive that you really like.

If you find that any of them might be transferable to your own situation, call up the organization that issued it. Ask how it performed and what the results were. They'll be pleased to tell you.

A pretty sure tip is that if the organization uses the same packages over and over again, it's getting good results.

Certainly, future and strategic planning are imperative. In today's world, there is no margin for catch-as-catch-can. But let there be no allowance, no tolerance for analysis paralysis. **Ready, Fire, Aim**—let that be your action credo.

On the basis of my experience, I feel that an organization's former CEO should not continue to serve on the board—except in rare cases and, at most, for a very short time.

Wit, Wisdom & Moxie

*I*n an organization, integrity permeates every aspect of its activity. It propels a singleness of purpose, purged of compromise or the search for material gain.

Don't be put off if you find out that one of your prospects has made a planned gift to another institution. Studies show that somewhere around 85 percent of those who have made a planned gift will make another one—either to your institution or somewhere else. And, of course . . . if they have already made a planned gift to your organization, there may be another one on the way. You can count on them being your best prospects.

The other day, I was reading the mission statement for the *Los Angeles Times*: "We improve the performance of society by enriching, inspiring, invigorating, and educating our diverse communities. We are a trusted voice, providing compelling information and superior products and services through a living partnership with our readers, advertisers, employees, and shareholders. We excel by investing in our people in a dynamic work environment thriving on integrity, mutual trust, innovation, creativity, and teamwork."

Note that the statement contains a total of only 60 words—not one of which is about "news."

A vigorous organization never feels it has arrived. Never feels comfortable. Knows that today's solutions are simply not good enough for tomorrow.

If you've been thinking that the Internet is an effective tool but mostly for small gifts—note this well.

In a Notre Dame campaign that went well over its goal with $1.2 billion reported, the largest gift was $35 million. We can tell you that the donor started with a $100,000 gift that came over the Internet.

The number of people who give online is increasing at an amazing rate. Count on it—in the future, your donors will write fewer checks. They will donate on your Web site, if you make it easy for them. Electronic Funds Transfer is the future and will begin augmenting and then taking the place of snail mail.

I have been telling our clients for months that they need to develop a strategy for raising funds through their Web sites. If you haven't taken this step yet, you'll be left behind.

"*Why bother . . . it's too new . . . it can't be done . . . it isn't practical." These mind-forged disclaimers are repugnant to the dynamic organization. Encrusted barnacles to be swept away with refreshing, imaginative ideas.*

They don't want to burden their children.

One of John D. Rockefeller's advisors urged him to start giving his money away. "It is rolling up like an avalanche that will crush you and your children and your children's children."

Andrew Carnegie made gifts amounting to $350 million before he died in 1919—a sum that would be worth about $3 billion in today's dollars. Bill Gates has always said that, like Carnegie, he will give away most of his fortune before he dies. He plans to make sure his children are well taken care of, but he doesn't want to leave them the burden of tremendous wealth.

I'm finding more and more men and women who will make certain their children are taken care of but leave most of their estate to charity or a foundation. They don't want to hamper their incentive, take away their motivation, and do irreversible harm by leaving their children and grandchildren too much. "My money is going to the charities I care about—where I can see first-hand the good it does," they tell us.

campaign goal is a dream with a deadline.

Here we go again! **Irv Sheffel** is a humble man, not of immense resources. He lives quietly in Topeka, Kansas. He recently made a gift of $1 million to the campaign for the Topeka Community Theatre.

The folks in Topeka gave him a very nice dinner of appreciation and in his acceptance speech he said, "I know my pledge is listed as a contribution, but from my point of view it is one of the best investments I have ever made. It brings far greater pleasure than any investing I have done for personal gain. It will bring lasting benefits, not just to me and my family, but to individuals of all ages throughout our community."

I've been talking about this for some time. Try it. Instead of talking to your friends and prospects about making a gift, suggest to them instead that they are making an investment—in people and in the community. Like Irv, they are investing in the future and in lives, and the dividends are beyond measure.

Wit, Wisdom & Moxie

*T*he wayside is filled with brilliant men and women who start with a spurt but lack the stamina and fortitude to finish. Their places are taken by those with ideas who never know when to quit.

Eight million men in this country have children younger than their grandchildren. Ponder that!

It's important . . . because our experience is that second wives have greater influence in driving the gift.

You've been told that a sure sign of significant potential dollars from your prospects is to measure the number of years they've been giving. Some say that may actually be more important than the number of dollars given.

I say: Take a different perspective. Don't track the dollars . . . chart instead the involvement and participation. Monitor their experiences, and offer additional opportunities of the right sort at the right time. You will deepen and greatly enhance the person's level of giving. And . . . the deeper the relationship, the more likelihood of your getting the major gift and then the ultimate gift.

Here's what you can count on: The more involvement, the greater the love. The greater the love, the more the giving. It's that basic.

*W*hen it comes to giving . . .
some people stop at nothing.

I've stressed how important it is that you get e-mail addresses for as many of your donors as possible. It's your future.

One way to do it that's obvious—is to request the information on the Return Envelope that carries the gift. You already ask for the donor's address, phone number, and how they want the funds used. Ask for their e-mail, also.

If they don't include it with their information, call them and ask for it. It's a great way to thank them again for their gifts.

Send out a questionnaire to your entire donor base and ask for their e-mail address. We did it recently and got over a seventy percent return. We thought the figure was high, perhaps skewed for some reason. It did go to a fairly sophisticated group of men and women. But you'll never know in your case unless you try.

*F*or the successful organization, there is a clanging discontent with conformity. The winning organization investigates. Seeks. Probes. Develops. Discovers. It teems with vigor, energy, and drive.

Some organizations wait for a campaign before writing a case. Don't wait! Its great value is that the case galvanizes staff, board, and giving constituencies to an unyielding focus and commitment.

Without it, the organization doesn't know where it's going . . . because there's no road map. See the Appendix for my "No Nonsense Guide to Help You Prepare a Statement of Your Case." It explains how to develop a perfect statement . . . and how to ensure its successful use.

Recently a national magazine advised its subscribers to review the IRS returns of any charity they wish to give to. This can be done at **www.guidestar.org**.

They'll find the 990 Form you filled out. It breaks down revenue sources, top salaries, even phone costs.

Be proactive. Invite donors to visit your 990 on the Web. Instead of a snooping expedition, make it a public relations coup.

*I*ntegrity is the thread that binds the organization's vision to its mission.

1 Your direct-mail package should not look or feel too expensive. That's not what captures attention. But the materials should be in keeping with the style and character of your institution.

2 Getting your prospect to open the envelope is your biggest challenge. Make certain it's compelling. They make a decision to open or to pitch in the first ten seconds of looking at the envelope.

3 They've opened the envelope and are now looking at your letter. That's great. Keep in mind—the first thing they look at is the P.S. Next, the signature. And after that, the first paragraph. If you haven't hooked them in the first paragraph, they won't go beyond that.

4 They spend as much time looking at the return card as they do the letter. Make certain the card contains an appeal as compelling, dramatic, and urgent as the letter. And be sure to ask for e-mail addresses.

5 A one-time appeal does very little to capture your prospect's attention and interest. Direct mail works best with multiple solicitations within a short period of time. "Get in their way"—that's what I recommend.

6 Segmentation is the key. Your 30-year-older and your prospect that is 70 have little in common. Neither do a lawyer and a teacher and a non-donor. Nor a doctor, a patient, a nurse. You must approach them differently.

They may all be wearing the same T-shirt, but they do not act or think alike. That means that your database has to work wonders for you, in some ways turn itself into a pretzel to give you the kind of segmentation you need. Pay attention to your infrastructure.

7 How do you like to receive an envelope with a label that is not fully typed or is at an angle? How about window envelopes? That's what I thought! Use regular envelopes. Get the typing right.

8 Personalize every opportunity you can. Call Mr. Jones, "Mr. Jones"—and if you know him well, "John." You've always known this and didn't have to be told—but repetition is good for the soul: a person's name is his or her most precious possession.

9 Spend a lot less time worrying about folding, stuffing, and getting the mailing out on time. Worry a lot more about the strategy of your mailing, the creation of the package, and then being able to evaluate it later. Go to a production house for all of that other stuff. It will pay off.

10 You've probably learned this the hard way. Successful copy is not written by a committee. Let three or four get ahold of your material—and you're sunk. Instead, have one person, perhaps the signer, read the material and approve it. Trust your own judgment— you've got style, savvy, and good common sense. You'll know best what works.

11 It's okay (in fact, I endorse the concept) to include an envelope with your newsletters. But make certain your newsletter achieves the objective of the newsletter—don't use it as a solicitation letter. Your newsletter should present the work and service of the organization in a compelling and dramatic way.

12 The world of direct mail is best not left to an amateur. Writing the perfect piece is one part an art and one part a science, mixed generously with an intuitive sense of what will work. There are plenty of folks around who are very good in this field. If the package is done perfectly, it will not cost you—it will produce a great deal of money.

*T*riumph is just **umph** added to **try**.

I've had a number of donors tell me in the past few months that they've received answering machine messages from some of our client organizations. They want to return the calls, but here's what they find particularly annoying.

Almost always, they recognize the name of the institution. The message is slow and distinct. But when it comes to the name of the caller and the phone number, it's so fast that even a court stenographer couldn't catch it. That means repeating the telephone message a second time. Even then it's tough to catch the name and number.

They won't repeat it a third time.

Studies show that organizations that send out regular mailings without an "ask" receive a higher rate of renewal and retention when the ask is actually made. And the more mailings that go out, the higher the renewal. Keep your donors regularly informed.

*F*ailure is not final or fatal. But not to make the attempt, that is the unredeemable failure.

I've been reminding everyone who will listen that it's important that you thank a donor **seven times during the year** for his or her gift. If you do, they will give again, and at a higher amount. I guarantee it.

It all starts with the first letter and expression of appreciation. Let me suggest the drill.

If you have the e-mail address (and, as I've said, you should), send an acknowledgment and appreciation immediately. Follow that with a receipt and a letter that is mailed within 48 hours.

Acknowledge the amount of the gift and indicate any previous contributions. It's important the donor understand that you recognize his or her ongoing support.

Let the donor know for what activity the gift will be used, review the importance of that particular activity, and express how grateful you are for his or her assistance.

Don't miss a single step in the process. If you do all of this, with the e-mail and the letter—you've already achieved two of your seven thank-yous!

*T*here are new frontiers to conquer. New markets to serve. New objectives to be achieved. Success is waiting, waiting for the organization responsive to unprecedented opportunities still unknown.

You may not be ready for this . . . but it's coming.

I've found that the fastest-growing format for "job performance evaluation" is the increasingly popular "360." This is the process in which you're rated not only by your boss, but also by co-workers, board members, and even donors.

Some who go through this evaluation come out feeling badly wounded. The "360" is done anonymously. Comments can be harsh, vengeful, and mean-spirited. But they can also be revealing.

A recent study shows that more people say they learn about planned giving and bequests through the published materials organizations distribute than from any other source. Keep reminding people of the importance of this form of giving. Keep sending the material.

A pig was complaining to a cow that he was not appreciated. "I don't understand it," he said, "people are always talking about how generous you are, giving the cream and milk and butter for their daily use. That's nice of course, but I give more than you do—ham and bacon and bristles and even feet. Yet nobody has any use for me. They make fun of me and call me a pig. I don't like it."

"Perhaps the difference," the cow replied after a moment's hesitation, "is that I give while I'm still living."

How do you get the wealthy to give? One of the nation's leading authorities on governance, organizational structure, and strategic planning for the nonprofit world is **Dr. James M. Hardy**. He cites a recent survey of wealthy people. "What would encourage you to give more?" they were asked.

The top answer: "confidence that the organization will use my money wisely" (69 percent). Next came "investing in an organization in which I have great passion" (65 percent). "Tax incentives" were cited by only 39 percent.

How do you spark passion? It's easy. Simply embrace your donors . . . in your institutional hug. Involve them in your program. Make them part of what you do!

Causes don't raise money. People don't raise money. People with compelling causes raise money. Your case has to have relevancy, dramatic and emotional appeal, and a sense of urgency. Of all of these factors, "A sense of urgency" is very likely the most significant and compelling factor.

Y*ou have not . . . because you ask not.*

Here's one of the most exciting and creative "thank-yous" I've heard of. I tell our clients: "You can't thank a donor enough." Emory University came close.

Jake Schrum, the president of Southwestern University, told me the story. When Wayne Rollins made a substantial gift to Emory, they wanted to find a very special way to show their appreciation.

They wanted a memento he could keep on his desk as a reminder. They fashioned a very special sculpture that was a flower vase. Officials at the University delivered a rose to Rollins's office every day. Every day for a year! Soon after, by the way, he gave an additional $40 million to name the business school.

If you use place cards at your board meetings to identify directors, print the name of the board member on the side facing out. On the side facing in . . . put your mission statement. (They don't need their name on the side facing them. They know who they are!) When trustees look at the mission statement during the meeting, they're reminded what their work is all about.

*E*xcellence is an organization's life-line. It is the most compelling answer to apathy and inertia. It unleashes a stimulating and pulsating force. Once it becomes the expected standard of performance, it develops a fiercely driving and motivating philosophy of operation.

Here's a good rule to follow . . . but only if you've been consistent in tracking and recognizing those who have indicated their estate plans for your institution. For every person who has told you about estate plans, you can count on 5 or more who have named you in their will, but have not told you.

It's important to get the names of these people, to keep them in your recognition and appreciation loop. The more you work at this, the more names you will identify.

Put your budget and your energy where there's the greatest payoff. To raise a dollar from special events, it costs $0.50 to $1.00 . . . from phonathons, $0.20 to $0.40 . . . from direct mail, $0.30 to $1.20 . . . and from personal solicitation and involvement of volunteers, it costs $0.07 to $0.15 to raise a dollar. That doesn't mean that direct-mail programs and special events aren't important . . . but only if they help you bubble-up the major donor.

A vision without proper planning is only a dream. Planning is the magic that makes great dreams come true. Planning and an intrepid determination to succeed can make the most audacious of objectives come true.

Wit, Wisdom & Moxie

LINCOLN'S GETTYSBURG ADDRESS
(As Revised by Members of the Board)

Something mystifying takes place when a group is asked to review or edit a case statement. It tends to kindle qualities in a person that are somewhere between sadism and belligerence. There's something uncontrollably satisfying in reworking material. Someone else's material! We understand that the feeling is very close to what pre-historic cavemen felt when they clubbed an enemy. What follows is a revision of the Gettysburg Address after a committee and board members were asked to look it over:

"Four score and seven years ago"
should be "eighty-seven years and four months ago"

"our fathers"
confusing . . . do you mean the Pilgrims, or those who signed the Declaration of Independence, or what?

"brought forth on"
"founded" would be a better

"this continent, a new nation"
be specific and name the country

"conceived in liberty"
sounds awkward . . . better say "based on the idea of freedom"

"and dedicated to the proposition that **all men** are created equal."
tsk! tsk! what about women? we can't afford to upset the women

"Now we are engaged in a great civil war, testing"
make this the first paragraph . . . taking too long to get into the story

"whether that nation or any nation"
not necessary. . . just say "our nation"

"so dedicated and so **conceived"**
there you go using "conceived" again . . . say "established"

"can **long endure."**
endure what? a better term would be "continue to exist"

"We **are met"**
mixed tenses, very bad . . . say "have met" or "are gathered"

"on **a great battlefield of that war."**
what battlefield? why not use the specific name?

"We have come to dedicate a portion of that field as **a final resting place** for those"
why beat around the bush? just say "cemetery"

"who here gave their lives **that that nation** might live."
"that that" sounds like "ratatat-tat" . . . how about "that our country"?

Sorry Mr. Lincoln, but you'd better try again. What we're after is something that's hard-hitting, with more punch. Something with some snap, crackle, and pop. More authoritative and forceful. Something impressive—something that people will read and remember! By the way, would you mind using a little better scratch paper? It's hard reading your notes from those used envelopes.

Donors want more information about how their gifts are being used. They want to know about results and outcomes. The good news is that this desire provides a great opportunity for you: contact your donors, get their views on how their gifts are being used, and ask for an increased donation. Try it! It works.

Take, for example, a gift of $1,000 to the Salvation Army. How many blankets will that buy, how many cups of coffee, how many overnights for homeless? How many hours of operation will it support? You get the idea. Our tests show the more specific the information you give, the better the donor likes it. The payoff: bigger gifts in future.

I once asked a group of corporate contribution decision-makers: Would you prefer to buy a table at our dinner for $1000, recruit eight people to sit at it, and let us use about half the money for our good cause? Or would you rather give us $1000 directly, let us use all of it for a good cause, and stay home with your family that night? What do you think was the response? You guessed right. Go for the $1000 gift.

*C*ount the ways you are blessed. Be thankful. Be slow to quarrel. Search out a forgotten friend. Suspend suspicion, be trusting. Write a love letter. Share a treasure. Give a soft answer. Encourage youth. Show your loyalty in word and deed. Nourish a grateful attitude. Keep a promise. Find the time. Don't harbor a grudge. Listen. Apologize if you are wrong. Be understanding. Be slow to envy. Forgive. Think first of someone else. Be kind. Count on miracles. Laugh more. Be gentle. Wage war against prejudice. Worship your God. Take pleasure in the beauty and wonder of the earth. Speak your gratitude. Speak it again. Speak it still again. Speak it still once more.

Never send a solicitor to make a call who has not already made his or her own sacrificial gift. The board must also give sacrificially. If they don't support the program, why should anyone else?

Michael Bloomberg's $50 million gift to Johns Hopkins puts him among the top philanthropists in the U.S. He offers sound advice: "When I'm asked for a major gift, my first question to the solicitor is, 'What did you and the organization's board members personally give?' If you and they don't support the cause, maybe it doesn't deserve my help. Not everyone can give large amounts, but a gift significant to the trustees' and requester's personal circumstances is a prerequisite to getting me interested. Conversely, when I ask others for money, I always start by describing my support. Those I'm asking have a right to know."

Note this well. In working with clients, I've become more and more aware that the truly successful organizations are guided by trustees who understand that it is not the resources that determine their decisions . . . It is their decisions that determine the resources.

A leader wages everlasting war on the status quo and mediocrity. A leader is an opportunity seeker and seizer. Receptive, curious, unafraid. There is a can-do spirit, uninhibited and unencumbered by the past.

Here's something new. Increasingly, I'm finding donors who *endow* their annual gift.

Say, for instance, that a donor has been giving $10,000 a year for the past few years . . . and wants to ensure that the gift continues in perpetuity or for at least some designated number of years. If the institution's endowment fund has been earning an average of 9 percent for the past several years, the donor gives $110,000 to the endowment—which sustains the annual gift.

Donors find this very appealing. Many continue their regular annual giving—plus the endowment.

Have a subcommittee talk about establishing a special *Perpetual Giving Society*. Have members of the group initiate the program with their own endowment. Your donors will love the concept.

Sell the dream and the vision. Donors give to the magic of the program. The large gifts are made viscerally, not cerebrally. Go for the magic. Make certain your case has emotional, dramatic appeal. Make it compelling and urgent.

An organization must make an intrepid covenant. Where there is no venture, there is no momentum. There must be an unrelenting quest for breaking the rigid shackles of institutional paralysis. Momentum compels a full effort and commitment, galvanized to the highest of ideals. There is an unending effort of heart and mind, soul and spirit.

We don't recommend *pledge cards*. Heresy? Not at all.

Research shows the word "pledge" has a negative connotation. Many donors don't want to be legally bound or make a commitment that encumbers their estate. That's especially true in difficult economic times.

Instead of pledge cards we use "gift cards." It may seem a trifling difference, but it works. And we don't use legally binding, or restrictive language.

Try using wording such as this: "I/we believe so strongly in the work of the Salvation Army and its wonderful service to those in need, that it is my/our intention over the next three years to give _____. If, for any reason at all, I cannot make a payment, I'll call the Army office. My payment will be forgiven or extended. I also understand this gift does not encumber my estate."

Surprise: Our attrition rate is less with the new wording. We use gift cards and we use letters of intent—a much more effective and personal way to extend a gift over a period of years.

Wit, Wisdom & Moxie

*G*reat opportunities surround us—
but escape all but the most vigi-
lant and diligent. There are no
trifling moments, no days without unending
return and rewards. The genius of life and
professional success is to capture the precious
opportunity.

Josh Weston is CEO of the $4 billion ADP Corporation—a major donor and a good corporate citizen. Weston heads a number of significant causes.

He says he reads every single request for a gift that comes to ADP—and there are plenty. "I don't leave something this important to others."

But here's the lesson. He says he can gauge a program's worthiness in the first two or three pages. If it's not there to seize his interest, he has a hard time wading through the rest of the proposal.

Listen to Weston! "Prepare a two or three page summary—and make sure it packs emotional impact and a sense of urgency. Early pages need to grab the reader by the lapels . . . and shake them."

How do you gauge the level of your ask? There are no set rules. But our research shows that a donor will not give more than 5 percent of his or her gross net worth for a major gift. And if it's their first major gift, it's more likely to be around 1 percent of their net worth, tops.

Wit, Wisdom & Moxie

There is not a right way to do a wrong thing. Something is either right or it is wrong. You must stand up for what is right, even if you are standing alone. It can be a scourging test of character. You do what is right—with resolve that is unwavering, unobstructed, and uninterrupted.

Nobody likes to do them . . . but Call Reports have to be done. They provide a paper trail, history, and continuity.

Don't try to take notes at your visit—unless it's something technical or is necessary for a planned gift. But immediately after the meeting, make notes of everything you heard and saw. Everything. No detail is too small . . . put it in the file. You'll find it invaluable for your next meeting.

Don't worry about the form being too formal or structured. That will kill it—slain by the sword of over-sophistication and structure. I recommend as simple a system as possible. In fact, let everyone do the report in a way that is most comfortable for him or her. As long as everyone does it.

And be certain to leave the kind of records that will be helpful and essential to the person who takes your place. Tomorrow you might be hit by a pie truck! Someone will need to pick up where you left off.

G ive your time to great causes. Let your candle burn at both ends if necessary. It will provide a dazzling light, a beacon for others to follow.

One effective way to thank your donors is to call to verify the spelling of their names for the listing in the Annual Report. Tell them, "This gives me a chance to thank you for your generous help . . . and all that you do for us. Your gift really means a great deal to us, and to all we serve."

If you feel you're too busy to make all those calls—what are you doing that's more important than thanking donors? If the staff is too busy to make calls, involve your volunteers. It's a great job for them . . . and they'll have a wonderful time.

The president of Prudential Insurance, **D. N. Pope**, believes in the law of averages. He says that in order to be successful you have to make the call and make contacts. He means at least 8 hours a day, maybe more. That's every day of the week, week after week. He tells fundraisers, "Make enough calls and you'll get the gift."

*I*f Columbus had turned back, no one would have blamed him. But no one would have remembered him either.

Wit, Wisdom & Moxie

Lessons from Geese

When a goose flaps its wings, it creates an "uplift" for the bird following. By flying in a V formation, the whole flock adds 71 percent more to its flying range than if each bird flew alone.

Lesson: A development staff and volunteer leaders who share a common purpose, commitment, and passion for the cause can get where they are going quicker and more successfully because they are traveling on the thrust of one another.

If a goose falls out of formation, it suddenly feels the drag and resistance of trying to fly alone. It quickly gets back into formation to take advantage of the "lifting power" of the bird immediately in front.

Lesson: Staff and volunteers know to stay in formation with those who have the proper direction and focus.

When the lead goose gets tired, it rotates back into the formation. Another bird takes its place at the point position.

Lesson: Staff and volunteers understand that it pays to take turns doing the hard tasks and sharing leadership. Even the lead goose knows it needs help at times.

The geese in formation honk from behind to encourage those up front to keep up their speed.

Lesson: Volunteer leaders need to make sure their "honking" from behind is encouraging and empowering.

When a goose gets sick or wounded or shot down, two geese drop out of formation and follow it down to help and give protection. They stay with the goose until it is able to fly again. Then they launch out again on their own and catch up with the flock.

Lesson: If staff and volunteers have as much sense as geese, they stand by each other—through the most difficult of situations and trying of times.

A title makes a difference. Sometimes a negative one.

Danny Rutland, VP of Mississippi College, says it was nearly impossible to schedule interviews when a member of his staff identified himself as "Director of Planned Giving." But when he simply said he was calling from the college and just wanted to come by for a visit, his batting average soared.

I also think a title like "Director of Major Gifts" is off-putting. It can be frightening for some people: "Who said I was a major gift prospect?"

With a little creativity, you can come up with something that causes less trepidation and caution from a prospective donor.

You can count on it. It's been tested, time and time again—it's been proven. In telephone and letter campaigns, if you encourage people to use a credit card when making a gift, your results improve dramatically.

*B*ecause of you, lives are being changed and saved. You are raising the funds necessary to provide the scholarships, heal the sick, take care of the abused, feed the hungry. It's because of you. You are as important in helping to cure cancer as the research scientist in the lab. You are doing it. And along the way, remember to have fun. If your work isn't fun, it's nothing.

When preparing your next direct-mail package, remember—spend half the time creating the reply form. Many waste too much effort on the sale, too little on the buy.

Be certain of one thing: After you have made your dazzling and compelling case for the prospect to give, make it very easy for them to respond. Donors spend as much time reading the return envelope as they do your glorious prose in the letter.

Stop calling them "annual gifts"! It makes it sound as if they're meant to be given only once every year. Here's what we know: if you ask your donor base to give a second time during the year, 40 percent will. Try it!

Instead of "annual gifts," give them a name that identifies them with your organization—scholarship gifts, Back-a-Youth gifts, Save-a-Life gifts. Change the name and your thinking and go after a second gift . . . for a special project the donor chooses.

The rules for success don't work unless you do.

Nothing beats networking as a way to engage and secure new donors. Cold calls are tough, but sometimes necessary.

Typically, of 100 fundraising cold calls, 50 individuals will not be around to take the call; 20 will ask you to call back; and ten will give a negative response. Only ten will agree to see you.

Still . . . it's not totally a lost cause. If you can get ten appointments from those 100 calls, and ultimately three gifts from those ten appointments— you're doing great. Those are three gifts you would not have gotten otherwise.

The choice is entirely up to you. Sit in your office waiting for lightning to strike, or make the 100 calls and get three gifts.

Your institution's Web site should include a section on philanthropy. If it doesn't, get busy immediately.

Make certain the page is emphatic about the opportunity to invest in changing lives and saving lives through your organization. Use a secure server to encourage online credit card donations.

Wit, Wisdom & Moxie

*P*roper planning determines the basic character of an organization—its mission, its willingness to implement, and its fervor for boldness.

You will want to share this story with your key people. **Chris and Warren Hellman** are active volunteers and philanthropists in the San Francisco area. She chairs the San Francisco Ballet. He heads Berkeley's $1 billion capital campaign.

When their children were in their early teens, the Hellmans funded a small foundation—enough that each of the three children had $15,000 a year to give to charities of their choice. The five family members comprised the board. All decisions for gifts had to be approved unanimously. The choices were fascinating and profound.

Today, the children are leaders in their communities. The philanthropic principles they learned at an early age were not lost. Today, they're heavily involved and are generous donors. The apple doesn't fall far from the tree . . . not if there has been careful nurturing and pruning.

Change your mindset. Men and women who seem obviously to have wealth are not necessarily your best prospects for major gifts and planned gifts. Your best friends are all around you. Probe a little, search, and cast your net.

I've read some wonderful direct-mail letters that are compelling, and tell a dramatic and appealing story about the work of the institution. But they never get around to actually asking for the gift. Or if they do, the ask is buried in the copy. I recommend:

When putting cheese in the mousetrap, always leave room for the mouse.

You know the tried and true rule that 80 percent of the money comes from 20 percent of the donors. Well . . . the 80/20 guideline has gone the way of the dinosaurs.

Several years ago, we began noticing that it was moving closer to: 90 percent of the money comes from ten percent of the donors. Now, it's even more skewed than that. In a recent study of 23 universities, I found that 97.4 percent of the money came from 1.7 percent of the donors.

Put your focus on major gifts—that's where the future is.

Start keeping a careful log of your time. Try it for two weeks. Determine how much time you should be spending on cultivation and how much time on actually contacting donors and asking for a gift. If your log doesn't measure up to your expectation, start making changes. To do that requires a real commitment on your part. I have an instrument to measure and help allocate your time. See "Time Allocation & Priorities" in the Appendix

*T*he difference between playing to win and playing not to lose is often the difference between success and mediocrity.

For the first time in its history, the U.S. is home to 100,000 men and women 100 years of age and older. The bad news is that these oldies tend to hold onto their money longer to insure their security. The good news is that there is a major increase in the number who are writing wills and making charitable bequests. Design a plan to reach these people . . . if you don't, some other organization will. You can count on it.

One thing more of particular interest. Those who provide for charity in their estate plans live longer than the general public—six years beyond the Actuarial Tables. (This gives some credence to the old fundraising homily: "No one lives as long as a widow who has left you in her will.")

Try this: Have informal pictures taken of your key donors, preferably with the children you serve, or professors, or doctors, at your site, and display them in your board room or at other prominent locations. Giving is about people, not plaques.

G*iving is the magic that gives life joy and meaning.*

Here's a great new annual giving idea. **Scott Asen** is chair of the $100 million capital campaign for Groton School, one of the "Ivy" Independents. But the concept he came up with deals with ongoing, sustaining giving.

It's called "The Founder's Club." To belong, each donor has to give a minimum of one percent of the annual giving goal. It also means that each year that the goal goes up, the member automatically increases the gift. So far, after three years, there's no attrition.

The name could have more pizzazz, but it's working—so who cares. Use the idea. Create your own name. It's a new twist—with a hook.

It won't get easier to raise money from corporations. In next ten years, 85 percent of labor force will work for companies which employ fewer than twenty people.

It's hard to get your arms around that small a unit.

Wit, Wisdom & Moxie

*T*he great dividing line between success and failure can be stated in six words: "I did not have the time."

Every charitable institution, whatever the size, should have regular programs to contact key donors and prospects. This can mean contact of one sort or another six to nine times a year.

If you devote your full time to planned or major gifts, with no other major assignments, your optimal number of prospects should be somewhere in the range of 125 to 175 persons. Add to this the very top donors you should be contacting regularly to maintain good stewardship.

Consult the Appendix for a grid that shows the number of contacts that should be made on a monthly basis. This form will be highly valuable in planning and evaluating your progress.

The increased cost of snail mail makes e-mail more attractive all the time. It exerts a quicker and greater impact on all donors—no matter what the age. (I'm finding that older men and women, over 70, are logging two to three hours a day on the computer.) Don't give up regular mail, but if you're not using e-mail, you're missing a bet.

*I*n fundraising, constant hard work is the yeast that raises the dough.

Claude Rosenberg, Jr., says the wealthy in this country can give $100 million more than they do now . . . and not miss it. He proves his point in a remarkable book called *Wealthy and Wise* (Little, Brown, 1994).

It's not a fast read, but its the kind of book you'll want to study and analyze—and put into the hands of board members and wealthy donors. Rosenberg's thesis is convincing. In Milwaukee, we had one donor who read the book . . . and increased her giving from $100,000 to $1 million.

This will surprise you.

Most men and women who make really large bequests are small annual givers. Experience shows that many who are very generous in death have given little or nothing in the way of lifetime gifts.

Here's the lesson: Pay attention to your lower level donors—there's a bequest in there somewhere.

*B*elieve in something bigger than yourself. Get involved in a bold and exciting cause.

Every study conducted and all the evidence I have demonstrates that those who give reserve their largest gifts for organizations with which they 1) are intimately acquainted and 2) have been involved for a substantial period of time—usually as a volunteer with board responsibility.

If you agree with this thesis—and it's irrefutable—why isn't your organization spending a priority of time and energy engaging men and women who can make a financial difference for your organization's future? If you're too busy to begin the process, you'll be on the losing side.

I'm finding that donors are more and more interested in what happens to their dollars. They're calling it an "investment" rather than a gift. They're a bit more skeptical and unsentimental. They demand to see frequent progress reports. They want results. They are impatient and insist on solutions and outcomes. They want to fast-forward cures in progress. They accept long-range goals, but are not motivated by them.

*B*lessed are the money raisers—and in heaven they shall stand on the right hand of the martyrs.

—John R. Mott

It's plenty tough to get prospects to read your mail! But there's a good chance your magnificent package won't even arrive.

Michael Critelli, CEO of Pitney-Bowes, tells me that a study authorized by his firm shows that 31 percent of third-class mail is not delivered. That's right—31 percent! Not delivered!

He says the reason is that the Post Office takes no responsibility for third-class mail, has no accountability regarding it, and doesn't even like the stuff.

Each local post office has jurisdiction over how third-class is handled. In some cities, it can sit around for weeks. And then, as the study discovered, it's still not delivered.

Bad news for all of us. It's hard enough to get the envelope opened, the message read, and the prospect moved to act. But if the mail doesn't arrive, your chances are less than winning the lottery.

S *ome irrefutable fundraising verities:*

1. *Every direct mail person has a scheme that will not work.*

2. *If a market research project is not worth doing at all, it is not worth doing well.*

3. *When it comes to staff, negative expectations yield negative results. Positive expectations yield negative results.*

4. *Regarding special events, the first 90 percent of the task takes 90 percent of the time. The last 10 percent takes another 90 percent.*

5. *If you have an impossible annual financial objective, and a Chair who is unreasonable, and a CEO who doesn't understand fundraising, remember the age-old dictum; to hell with the cheese; get out of the trap!*

You're not going to like this . . . but it won't be a surprise. In a survey of the 130 major corporations in the country, 91 percent slashed budgets last year, laid off employees, or underwent some other changes. The result: major restructuring of their giving programs.

Today, companies tie their giving to the business they do. They design grant programs that will be of financial worth to them. In the future you will have an increasingly difficult time getting a corporate gift if there isn't a direct payoff for the company.

One major camp found a way to thank donors that paid tremendous dividends. The camp had their "scholarship kids" attach their photographs to drawings they had made. The drawings and photos were delivered to every donor of $500 or more . . . in person. The renewal rate of these people soared to 97 percent . . . and dollars the following year rose threefold.

The same technique will work for a scholarship YMCA camper, a student at a school, a grateful abused child at a shelter, a recovering teenage drug addict. You get the idea.

Wit, Wisdom & Moxie

Do all the good you can,
By all the means you can,
In all the ways you can,
In all the places you can,
At all the times you can,
To all the people you can,
As long as you ever can.

—John Wesley

Invite a client to every board meeting for a five- to ten-minute report on how effectively the organization has served. Don't worry about it taking too much time away from the important items on the agenda. This could very well be the most important item! It will remind directors of what the organization is all about.

But here's something special. I heard for the first time a major donor who reported to the board about why she had made her large gift, one of the largest in the history of the organization. Why hadn't we thought of this before! It was electrifying. It was one of the biggest boosts the directors had ever had. And the donor felt great about being able to tell her story.

Taft School (Watertown, Connecticut) set a campaign goal recently of $75 million—and ended up raising $133 million.

Here's what's important about the numbers. Ninety-three percent of the campaign total came from 200 donors.

*M*ore church bulletin bloopers I
have read:

1. Tonight's sermon: "What is Hell?" Come
   early and listen to our choir practice.

2. For those of you who have children and
   don't know it, we have a nursery down-
   stairs.

3. Remember in prayer the many who are
   sick of our church and community.

4. Potluck supper: prayer and medication to
   follow.

5. Don't let worry kill you off—let the
   church help.

I haven't heard of anyone who has put their auction online. I think it's a great idea—if you've tried it, let me know.

Sell tickets to participate, and show items off to their best advantage. Silent bidding on everything, and a week to participate.

The biggest payoff of all: Let everyone know that you're giving them an evening at home. They ought to pay plenty for that.

R ichard Grant, director of the Dan Murphy Foundation (Los Angeles), tells me he can't recall ever receiving a thank-you letter—from an organization that his foundation turned down.

This is something you should do. It's a courtesy to thank the foundation staff for considering your proposal. It's also smart. The letter is the first step toward the next proposal.

Do the same with individuals. It pays off!

*T*o grasp every opportunity is to embrace the whole of life. For leaders who seize the moment—earnestly, eagerly, persistently, and with zeal—it is these resolute men and women who realize the greatest achievement and the richest fulfillment and reward from their work.

Martin Luther King said: "The time is always right to do what is always right." Do it now.

Multiply your annual budget by three. That's the absolute minimum you should have in your endowment. I tell my clients it should be three to five times the annual budget—but let's take the minimum. If it's less, your institution is seriously subject to the vagaries of the economy. If the economy dips, you may find your institution sliding as well.

Here's what to do. Project what your annual budget will be three years beyond the current fiscal year. Multiply that figure times three. That should be the minimum in the endowment fund. If you're not there—start doing something about it. Now!

There's whole world out there interested in your cause. You must identify and talk to them about your own great work!

How do you calculate the appropriate gift for senior staff to make to the organization's capital campaign? First of all, the chief executive officer and the chief development officer should certainly lead the way. Use as your guide that, spread over a five-year period, they should give ten to 15 percent of their annual salary.

*E*ach time a man stands up for an ideal, or acts to improve the lot of others, or strikes out against injustice, it sends forth a tiny ripple of hope.

—Robert F. Kennedy

I oppose the idea of criticizing another organization. It's wrong, it's futile, and the donor doesn't like it.

People will support you if they believe in your mission. If they give enthusiastic support to another organization, congratulate them on their involvement and their philanthropy. Then move on to another prospect.

There's whole world out there interested in your cause. You must identify and talk to them about your own great work!

It's very hard to make gift acknowledgment letters seem personal. That's true of even those you prepare individually. The canned ones are even worse.

Nothing beats including a handwritten note—even with a boilerplate letter. It means you cared enough to pull out the letter and add a personal touch and thought.

A dozen words or so will do: "Your gift means so very much to us and those we serve. I can't thank you enough."

*I*t is every man's obligation to put back
into the world at least the equivalent
of what he takes out of it.

—Albert Einstein

Here's a truly inspired way to say thank you. It's a win-win for everyone.

One of my clients invited a foundation executive to a board meeting to explain why the foundation decided to make a grant to the organization. It was an eye-opener for the board and a great way to affirm the organization's value. Hearing the high praise from an outsider, particularly a foundation executive, was very special for board members.

The meeting ended with the board giving the foundation executive a standing ovation. A wonderful way to say thank you to the foundation and an impressive session for the foundation executive.

Every organization should provide donor categories or clubs whose benefits increase with the donor's level of giving. It will help insure increased donations.

Aim high because certainly some in your constituency will want to contribute at the highest level. Limit your categories to five. Anything more than that will look like a smorgasbord.

*M*oney is like muck—not good except if it's spread around.

—Francis Bacon

There's no guarantee the recipient will open your beautiful direct-mail package. Studies show that you have **eight seconds** to get the recipient to make the decision to open the envelope.

Swoosh. Will it end in the wastebasket or not? Is it addressed correctly, label or not, proper middle initial? Is there an identifiable return address?

If everything is okay and the outside package looks enticing, a decision is made to open the envelope. Now the battle begins. Will they read the message or not?

Here's an effective and very easy way to test your letter the next time you do a direct-mail program. Divide your total list into three. Send a different letter to each of the three groups . . . but keep everything else in your direct-mail package the same. That way, you'll be measuring the success of each letter. You'll be able to see which draws the very largest response.

No easy task, this. Raising funds can be demanding, often frustrating, at times unforgiving. Early on, the fundraiser makes the decision: What shall I do with my life? How much will I sacrifice? How much am I willing to give of myself, my time, my love, my energy— indeed, my life? You decided, and you find that life has taken on a new meaning, exhilarating beyond belief and filled to the brim with rewards and fulfillment incalculable.

His days of giving "go-away" gifts, even to friends, are over, **Jim Rogers** tells me. (Jim has given away over $300 million.)

By "go-away" gifts, he means those he makes not because he believes in the solicitor's organization—but just so the solicitor will go away.

He says he will only give now when he sees real advances being made by the organization. He wants to believe strongly in the mission of the organization he supports. He wants to feel deeply involved in the organization's work.

It probably happens to you all the time—someone tells you that they have already put you in their will. This is great news. But while a bequest may be a very special arrangement for some folks, it may make more sense for them financially to make the gift while still alive. This is especially true when appreciated assets are present.

By the way, if you probe just a little bit, you'll find that friends of your organization will be quite free in telling you that they have included the organization in their will and for what amount. Just ask!

It is one of the beautiful compensations of this life that no one can sincerely try to help another without helping themselves.

—Charles Dudley Warner

Wit, Wisdom & Moxie

Fund-raiser/fund raiser/fundraiser: One word or two? How about a hyphen?

Let's solve this by using none of the above.

When the term refers to a development officer, it distorts the meaning of philanthropy. Giving is not about a fundraiser—or a development officer, or a consultant. It's about a worthy cause, a generous donor, an effective volunteer.

When an organization needs money it may say, "Let's hire a fundraiser." Wrong! Better to say, "Let's examine our case, let's cultivate our constituency, let's recruit leadership. Then, maybe, we can get a professional to do the easy part, to get us organized, to help us harvest. But this person won't raise the funds—the organization will, the leadership will, the donors will."

Sometimes the term will refer to an event, as if an event by itself raises money. Again, the focus is misplaced; it suggests that the mission is to throw a party.

Well . . . let's explore the question. You know the question: Is it one word, two words, or hyphenated! There's an infallible rule that governs precisely the situation. If it's an adjective, it's one word: fundraising. If it's a noun, two words: fund raising. Or is it the other way around? In any case, I'm certain that the rule is inviolate.

Just for the record—I like to see it always as one word, no matter how it's used: fundraiser, fundraising. No hyphen, no slash mark, no space!

I called some people I consider authorities in our field. I spoke to one of the senior officers at AHP. She told me that she really wasn't sure how it was handled at headquarters: "We have no real policy about that and I guess each staff person handles the word as he or she chooses. I think I usually use two words for both the noun and the adjective. I'm not sure about the verb. I guess two words, also."

I called Dick Wilson. Wonderful Dick Wilson—for years he was executive director for the NSFRE (AFP). He always knows about this sort of thing.

Wit, Wisdom & Moxie

"Dick, I have a serious problem. Is it fundraising (one word), fund raising (with a space), or fund-raising (with a hyphen)?"

There was a long pause. "I make it two words all the time. But hold on a minute. We have a glossary around here somewhere that we printed a couple of years ago that governs that sort of thing. We felt that we needed a rule so that everyone will know the proper thing to do. There's been a lot of confusion about this word. Let me see if I can find a glossary."

Dick was silent for a long time. He finally returned. "Well, I'll be darned. In the glossary we say the word should be hyphenated all the time—for a noun, adjective, or a verb. I guess I've been doing it wrong all this time."

"Well, do you think you will change?"

"I guess I'll keep doing it the way I have."

I rather agree with Dick. Glossary or not, seeing the word hyphenated just somehow doesn't look right to me.

I knew what to do. I called my dear friend, John J. Schwartz. For years, Jack was president of the AAFRC, one of the nation's leading spokesman on fundraising (or fund-raising, if you have a bias towards the glossary). If anyone would know, Jack would. I have never known him to equivocate on anything.

"Well, Jack, I have this problem." And I explained my dilemma.

There was a long pause. In this investigation, I've learned a lot about long pauses!

"To tell the truth, I don't know if there is a rule about this sort of thing and I don't believe anyone is really consistent about it."

"How do you handle the word, Jack?"

"Well I use two words, but that's just my preference. Let me see if I've got any material around here." And another long pause. "Well, this is interesting. Here's a piece from AAFRC where's it's hyphenated and there's an article in a magazine where it's two words, and here's a folder where they use it both ways." We spoke some more and finally decided that I probably ought to make it two words. That seemed to make the most sense.

About twenty minutes later, I had a telephone call. It was Jack Schwartz. He said he had just checked with the office at AAFRC and there's definitely a rule in the style manual. "The word—whether it's a noun, an adjective, or a verb—is to be hyphenated."

Good grief. I just don't like that hyphen!

So I called my publisher and reported the puzzle and the results of my investigation. He somehow didn't feel the same kind of passion for the matter that I did.

"Aaron," I said, "it seems to me that no one really knows, and I definitely don't like the hyphen. Let's decide what to do. The important thing, Aaron, is that we be consistent.

"Let's make the noun and the adjective one word. I really like it that way and it looks good to me. And let's hyphenate the verb."

It really didn't matter a lot to me, hyphenating the verb. I don't use it very much—in fact, I seldom use it as a verb. Well, I just tried it—and I still don't like that hyphen.

So I said to Aaron: "The important thing is to be consistent. Nouns, adjectives, verbs—they're all one word. No hyphens."

In the matter of two words, one word, or hyphenated—I suggest you choose your own style. Just be consistent. Follow Sally Rand's dictum. This is how the famous fan dancer explained her immense success: "I owe it all to the two most important rules of advertising that governed my life: always be consistent and follow the principle of using plenty of white space."

Wit, Wisdom & Moxie

*T*he fundraiser brings many talents and skills to the profession. But I can assure you that integrity is the mightiest weapon in your arsenal. Its power is explosive. It brings together uncompromising individualism and blinding honesty. And it must be combined, too, with compassion. For without grace and love, integrity is without heart and spirit.

Take a cue from Wake Forest University's thrust into e-mail.

Last year, when they sent an e-mail reminder to donors who had not renewed that year, three out of every ten sent in a check.

Two years ago, a graduate who lived overseas had not been in contact with the University for a half a dozen years. He found them on the Web site and sent an e-mail message. There was a response, of course. One thing led to another and when the alum visited the campus, he stopped by and dropped off a check for $40,000. And promised more.

The documentation is impressive. You need put more emphasis on the electronic world of fundraising.

A comment I overheard at a recent Council for Independent Colleges conference is not bad advice for any organization: the board empowers . . . the staff designs and implements . . . and the president leads.

Wit, Wisdom & Moxie

*D*ream the unthinkable, attempt the impossible. Be audacious. It is the magic of the idea that will lead your organization to victory.

I consider the following one of the best mission statements I have read. Just over 100 words (most no more than two syllables), beautifully written, completely understandable, and with powerful impact:

"We believe in the creation of inspired lives produced by the miracle of hard work. We are not frightened by the challenges of reality, but believe that we can change our conception of this world and our place within it. So we work, plan, build, and dream. We believe that one must earn the right to dream. Our talent, discipline, and integrity will be our contribution to a new world. We believe we can take this place, this time, and this people—and make a better place, a better time, and a better people. With God's help, we will either find a way, or make one."   —Providence–St. Mel (Chicago)

If your organization sponsors an annual summer golf tournament . . . save photographs of foursomes from the previous year—and send them out to the members just before Christmas, along with a little note and a "save the date" card. A great way to send a holiday greeting and a thank you, and nail down the date for next year.

I deem it the duty of every man to devote a certain portion of his income for charitable purposes; and that it is his further duty to see it so applied as to do the most good of which it is capable.

—Thomas Jefferson

We can probably never get away from gift clubs, plaques, and walls of honor, but we do have to try to add more personal recognition.

About gift club names: stay away from names such as founder, patron, benefactor, sponsor, investor. They are too generic and mean different things in different organizations. One cartoon shows a distinguished elderly gentleman talking to a friend in his club: "It got quite nasty, Eustis, as I was forced to remind the impudent fellow that I was a benefactor, not a patron."

Instead use names of prominent people in your organization's history, or landmarks, or words associated with what you are all about: The John Thompson Society, The Oak Tree Partnership, Health Associates, The Hospital Trust, The Board of Believers, The Fowler Avenue Regulars, The Children's Trust.

*P*hilanthropy is the mystical min-
gling of a joyous giver, an artful
asker, and a grateful recipient.

—Douglas M. Lawson

Outsource everything you possibly can. I'm really a big believer in that.

But when it comes to telemarketing, our studies show that when outsiders make the call, it seems to be a dead giveaway and donors don't like it.

You'll also find there's a good bit less irritation from those who get the calls if they know that it's from a student or someone on your staff.

There are lots of books on planned giving—but none better than **Debra Ashton**'s. Her book is out of print now and impossible to find. We keep our copy locked in our library! But she's working on a new one that should be out soon.

Debra cautions against cultivating prospects too long. She says that building relationships is important—but don't forget the ultimate goal. If you're visiting the same people year after year and still haven't brought up the subject of the gift, you're likely wasting time.

The organization that doesn't plan for the future is on a stormy, turbulent journey—destination unknown. The race is frenzied and explosive. There are new markets, different concepts, new and aggressive competition. Without proper planning an organization is without rudder or direction.

I've conducted several focus groups to determine how good the copy, layout, and design were in some of our campaign brochures and case statements. (Reaction was mixed, but mostly good!). And how folks like a layout and design.

I was surprised by one thing. The participants all said that what was missing were captions beneath the photos. Even photos that seemed self-explanatory.

I never thought we needed captions before. Now I know we do. And you know what—it's a plus! It's a great way to grab readers by the lapels and shake them. If captions weren't important, newspapers and magazine wouldn't be using them.

Bad news for direct-mail programs.

The Polk Company asked more than 18 million consumers nationwide to indicate which kind of direct mail they would and would not like to receive. Of the 6.7 million respondents, nearly two million opted out of nonprofit direct mailings.

The greatest problem with volunteers is not killing them with overwork, but simply boring them to death. Causes don't need workers as much as they need informed, dedicated, and passionate advocates.

—Harold J. Seymour

What words do you use to present your organization? Too often we use arcane terminology and dare the public to understand. Universities have chancellors and provosts and deans. Hospitals have residents and PICUs and MRIs.

Not very donor-friendly. Maybe even arrogant.

Especially when it comes to requesting support. You call the gift income officer the "Development Director." "Development" means something entirely different in the business community—why encourage confusion? Probably worse is "Director of Institutional Advancement." What does that mean to an outsider?

Here's a good way to estimate how much one of your regular donors will give to your big capital campaign. Take ten percent of their annual income. Spread that amount over a five-year period. Let's say their annual income is $200,000. That means a $20,000 gift spread over five years—$4000 a year. That's one yardstick you can use.

Y*ou cannot take with you in the hereafter what you haven't already given away.*

I'm a strong advocate of the concept of rotation for board members—three three-year terms, then one year off. Two three-year terms do even more to assure effectiveness, vitality, and zeal for the cause—while preventing the myopic stagnation of those who long for the good old days.

On the other hand . . . you mustn't lose a really effective and dedicated board member. If he or she must rotate off, find a way to keep that person engaged in some meaningful relationship and assignment. If you don't, another nonprofit will.

I am convinced that the most precious gift your organization can receive is a board member who is dedicated and devoted to the institution. In order to assure that board members understand their responsibilities, we recommend a "contract" between the organization and each board member. This assures a high level of commitment, enthusiasm, and advocacy for the organization. See the Appendix for a sample Statement of Understanding that clearly identifies the responsibilities of both the board member and the organization. It will ensure that you have the most effective board possible.

*T*here are some in fundraising who aim at nothing—and hit it with remarkable precision.

Shoot for a million dollars!

I tell my clients to be certain to evaluate their special events. Chances are almost certain that they are not generating sufficient funds to make up for the time invested. And that business about "friendraising"—every test I conduct indicates it's simply not true.

But here's a twist. Enlist a special task force to investigate the possibility of a mega event that will generate $1 million. Members of the task force need not be board members. What you need are free-wheeling, creative men and women, wildly imaginative types, who don't know what can't be done.

The concept is perfect if you organization is planning a major anniversary—but don't wait for that.

Don't say it's impossible for you to raise a million dollars. That will put you on the losing side. Go for it. The worst that could happen is that you come up with a number of good ideas, but they simply aren't realistic or won't work in your situation.

*V*olunteers are your organization's most precious asset. After the verb **to love, to help** is the most beautiful word in the language.

Red Cross leads the way in Internet fundraising. Your organization better get on board.

In 2001, even before September 11, the Red Cross was on track to raise over $9 million online in regular contributions. This compares to only $172,000 several years ago.

As far as a crisis is concerned, Red Cross officials learned that its donors like being able to contribute immediately after a disaster strikes. For that reason, they devote resources to making certain that their Web page is frequently updated with breaking news. They find that it is just as effective for raising current funds that aren't disaster-related.

This won't surprise you, but in many respects, sophisticated philanthropists are much like their for-profit investor counterparts. They tend to be risk-aversive and return oriented. (Read that: results-oriented.) This doesn't mean that your prospects avoid spontaneity or innovation— but I've found that you'd better know your prospects quite well before you make an adventurous ask.

The more I make, the more I can give away. The good Lord has been good to me and I'm trying to return the favor.

—Milton Pentrie

Select the right person for the job. Experience has told me that's where it starts. When you choose a new person for a fundraising position, spend as much time as possible to make sure you're making the right choice. Once that's done, establish appropriate and mutual expectations. Measure the new employee's objectives and results on a quarterly basis.

Work at keeping the person motivated and developing—as a person and a professional.

Keep in mind that people don't change. Not very much. Be certain not to hire someone with the thought that you'll be able to change them. It doesn't happen. You can't teach an old rat to kiss a cat!

If you find that you've made a poor choice, take action as soon as possible. My experience is that warnings don't help. They only delay the inevitable. In all of my years with over 1500 clients, I find few who change. That's why making the right choice to begin with is so essential.

Hire wisely, establish objectives, monitor and measure, motivate, and if necessary make a change promptly.

Nothing lifts your spirits or fills your heart more than giving your support and time to a great cause.

—John J. Schwartz

Count your expectancies.

I encourage clients to list their "expectations" on the development department's financial statements that are shown to the board. Don't tell me that they don't meet accounting standards. I know they don't!

Don't let the accounting department tell you what is best and most effective for the development office. You know of some who have left gifts in their estate plans—you have already enrolled them in your legacy society. We encourage you to ask them what they have given. Most will tell you.

List the amount actuarially so that board members can tell when the organization might expect certain amounts in the years ahead. It provides some comfort for the future, but more than that, it's a reminder of how very important estate planning is to the organization.

*I*f you want to know the value of an individual, ask not what the sum of all that he owns but look instead to the total of all he has given.

—Douglas K. Freeman

I have worked with a lot of designers. I have found that the really effective designers understand they're not designing brochures for you. Their designs are for your market constituency. That understanding is what makes a true talent.

The designer isn't interested in your likes and dislikes. They want to know everything there is to know about your prospects.

The great designers understand psychology, and they know persuasive techniques that compel your prospects and donors to act.

They understand that what might look "pretty"— and may even win an award—isn't necessarily what is best to meet your needs or raise the most money.

A recent study shows that bequests still account for seven out of ten of all of the planned gift types. That makes it all the more important to emphasize estate planning. And that makes it all the easier for even a small shop, without much planned giving sophistication, to promote what will be of greatest benefit to them— bequests.

Wit, Wisdom & Moxie

I tell the solicitors I coach that they should be prepared—they won't get every gift they ask for. You win some, you lose some. But no matter what the outcome, they will forever be, to use Ernest Hemingway's salute: "The winner and still the undisputed champion."

Don't wait for your quarterly newsletter to report the news. For some things, immediacy counts.

Take independent schools and small colleges, for instance. Typically, they foster very close relationships within classes. If a class member dies, or changes a job, or receives an honor, alums should be notified quickly and effectively. Classmates will want to know right away. Having an effective e-mail base of addresses assures a prompt way to be in contact.

The same concept can be applied to most organizations. Think of how you can use e-mail to get important messages to your friends and donors.

Be creative. It pays off.

Penn State, for instance, has 16 endowed positions for its football team. The endowed scholarships go for $250,000. That's plenty attractive—a bargain compared to the cost of endowing a chair in some dusty old academic department!

Wit, Wisdom & Moxie

*F*or most donors, the span between the head and the heart is a very short distance. But for some prospects, it's an unending journey that never reaches its destination.

Harvard University is taking a good look at e-mail.

I found out the other day that to examine the response from alums, Harvard sent a series of e-mail messages to a small test group. The response was much larger than their attempts at direct mail. They even had one who said, "I only want to be solicited by e-mail"—and he sent a $10,000 gift.

The university will soon allow donors to transfer stock electronically. It's something you should consider, also.

Saint Jude's in Memphis sends out eight mailings a year to their current donors—and a large number of the recipients make an additional gift each time they get a mailing. If you have a loyal group, try testing the concept of multi-mailings to those who already give. They care greatly about your work and mission—don't assume that they won't get great joy from making a number of gifts.

We make a living by what we get, but we make a life by what we give.

—Winston Churchill

I shared 50 direct-mail packages with a group of men and women. I made no attempt to make the composition diverse or average from an economic or educational standpoint. These were just regular men and women, precisely the kind of folks who receive your direct-mail packages.

I asked them what they liked and what they didn't. What caught their eye, and what turned them off. Here's what really surprised me. When they reviewed the material, they found that the weakest part of the message by far was actually "the ask."

The stories were great, by and large—compelling and dramatic. A number of the pieces expressed a sense of urgency (but not enough, in my opinion). But when it came to the ask, it was often weak, ho-hum, and in some cases, apologetic. Six out of 50 packages actually never even got around to asking for a gift, not directly.

Make certain your ask is relevant, dramatic, compelling, and urgent. It has to be clear and unambiguous. Don't forget, your object is not to tell a story—it's to get the gift.

Waiting until everything is perfect before making the call is like waiting to start a trip until all the traffic lights are green.

No easy task, being a board member. It should not be taken lightly. Perhaps foremost in importance is hiring and keeping precisely the right CEO. Evaluate the work of the CEO on a regular basis, and keep raising the bar. You will want the very best for the organization. And if you have the right person, choke him or her with gold.

A good board member understands thoroughly the mission of the organization, has passion for its work, makes certain there are sufficient funds so that there is not a "mission deficit," and insists on holding a steady course. Having the right CEO assures that all this happens.

Your board is your greatest asset. Spend ten or 15 minutes of each meeting on member responsibilities and policies. Put a board member in charge of this task and plan carefully, down to the minute. It should be a learning experience that is fun and inspiring at the same time.

Raising money takes dogged persist-ence, bullheadedness, salesman-ship, year-round cultivation, board support and encouragement, a plan, an attainable goal, and lots of excitement.

—Brian O'Connell

Try *dictating* your next direct-mail letter. Go ahead, do it!

Speak to your donors as if you were in their living room with them or talking over coffee. Be quick, off the cuff, spontaneous. After you have typed it all up—that's when you can begin honing your words. You'll add *snap, crackle, and pop* to your message. For now, just start a free-running flow and don't worry about grammar or context. You can take care of all that in your revision.

You've had it all wrong!

The color and texture of the paper you use have no effect on the results of your mailing. Nor does the use of blue versus black in the signature.

There's more that might surprise you. Metered mail does not draw better than mail bearing a bulk-rate indicia. And using the back and front of a single sheet draws as well as using two separate sheets. If it's an environmental organization, front and back is even more effective.

*T*here is one word that blocks action. The word derails momentum. It poisons motivation and chokes any chance for success. That killer word is: **can't**.

76 million baby boomers will have turned 50 this past year. This generation represents one of the most influential phenomena in the history of this country. Boomers are self-absorbed, leisure-loving, and doggedly skeptical.

They're also passionate about the things for which they care greatly. And remember, this is the generation that will be recipient to the $11.4 trillion that will be passed on to them from their parents.

Better begin now . . . to identify . . . interest them in your program and get them into your institutional hug.

U se *one* signature in your direct-mail piece rather than two or more. This is important.

To begin with, two signatures are much less effective than one. They decrease the vitality and warmth of the piece. And, worst of all . . . it makes the reader think that the letter was written by a committee. The recipient knows it isn't personal.

I love the word **compelling**. I believe your written word should be compelling, the ask should be compelling. It's a beautiful word. Compelling comes from the Latin words **com** (meaning "together") and **pellere** (meaning "to get or bring about by force and power").

Your organization's **purpose**, its mission, is a covenant, an uncompromising commitment to do something. When you put these words together, and create a **compelling purpose**, you provide the energy and magic that can achieve any objective.

Every organization should ask, what is its compelling purpose?

It's not what you think.

A fundraising letter is not an appeal from a non-profit, describing its needs and requesting a charitable gift to fill them.

Note this well. **An effective fundraising letter is an appeal from one person to another.** It describes an opportunity for the recipient to meet personal needs by supporting the cause. And it invites the recipient to take specific and immediate action.

When you write a fundraising letter, make sure you know precisely to whom you're writing. And why. Be certain your letter makes that point just as clear to them as it is to you.

You may be using the wrong approach. It's proven that when you insert a brochure in a prospect package, the results are almost always depressed. Yes, *depressed*!

*A*lways remember there's no 'ceiling' on philanthropy. In short: keep asking, keep raising sights, keep the heat on—because the money is there.

—George A. Blakely, Jr.

Here's an idea that pays double dividends. Major donors—individuals and foundations—are very interested in helping young people understand the spirit, traditions, values, and practice of philanthropy.

Develop programs in which you work with grade school children on their giving, conduct funshops about philanthropy. Let your majors know what you're doing.

Involve young people in your campaigns. For instance, in one of our Girl Scout campaigns, we asked for 100 percent participation from the scouters, and almost got it—6000 gifts in all. For some, it was only pennies. But that was okay. We helped foster the cause of philanthropy. But the big payoff came when we called on a foundation and showed them the computer list of 6000 names, the girls who had given personal gifts. It doubled the amount the foundation was thinking of giving.

Winners are those who make a habit of doing the things losers never take the time to do.

How do you rate against the record of Saint Jude's in Memphis?

When someone makes a pledge as a result of the St. Jude's telecast, 75 percent of those who call in actually fulfill their commitment. That's high. Those who call in on the 800 number receive a letter of thanks and a reminder within 48 hours. If there isn't a response, they get another reminder in two weeks—just a gentle, soft follow-up. After the gift is made, St. Jude's places donors in an eight-mailing cycle to encourage additional gifts.

Put your arms around those older donors.

People 55 and older are the fastest-growing sector of the personal computer–purchasing public. Seven out of ten seniors own a computer and use the Internet. Currently, 65 percent of those 55 years of age and older invest online. The same percentage have the potential to make their gifts over the Internet. Prepare now.

I often leave a session with a prospect wishing I had responded to a question differently. Or thinking of a better way I could have made the ask. Or even wanting to do the presentation all over again.

*The French have a wonderful phrase that expresses my frustration: **esprit d'escalier**. It describes the strike of inspiration that hits you as you reach the bottom of the staircase—when you realize what you should have said by way of a devastating retort.*

Getting gifts from doctors has always been . . . well, rather painful. But now, in California, it may become even more difficult medicine to swallow.

One-third of the state's 350 medical networks have closed their doors or declared bankruptcy. This leaves doctors with hundreds of millions of dollars in unpaid claims.

These networks were meant to be the middlemen between physicians and HMOs. Now they've left the doctor holding the medicine bag.

Your donors are probably online.

Here's what my studies show. Among university alumni under 40, 100 percent are online. For grads 40 years of age to 59, 97 percent have access to the Web. Virtually all have an e-mail address.

But here's something even more impressive. 80 percent of the alumni 60 years of age and over both have e-mail and make frequent use of the Web.

You shouldn't be disappointed if you fail. That happens. The great failure is not to have made the attempt.

It takes hard work. The dictionary is the only place where **success** comes before **work**. I always ask myself: "What great things would I attempt if I knew I could not fail?"

In the testing I have done, the word "pledge" received a negative rating. It is considered a pejorative term. Next lowest was the word "contribution." When you ask a person to share in your work, either verbally or in writing, don't ask for a contribution. It's a cold, brittle term.

Use the word "gift." It has a very positive connotation. It feels warm and good.

But best of all, try using the word "investment" or "invest." This meets with the greatest success: "We would like you to consider an investment in those we serve. The dividends will produce incalculable growth." Use your own words and rhythm, but you get the idea.

Debra Ashton, one of the most significant voices in planned giving, tells me she thinks she has spent too much time studying tax-saving techniques and not enough time building relationships with prospects and donors. She says that a planned giving officer should devote 95 percent of his or her time to building confidence-filled relationships and five percent to the "how" of making a gift.

*T*he prospects never looked brighter and the problems never looked tougher. Anyone who isn't stirred by both of those statements is too tired to be of much use to us in the days ahead.

—John W. Gardner

I have been urging you to get e-mail addresses for as many people as possible in your database.

But it can't end there. The bad news is that one out of three will change his or her e-mail address every year. That's more often than people change their mailing address.

It gets even more difficult. Donors tend to let you know when they change their mailing address, but seldom do for their e-mail.

It's a tough and takes effort to keep up with it— but it's essential. And worth it.

Robert Gilder is an investment manager and a philanthropist. He knows a thing or two about philanthropy. He cautions us: "Giving is as tough a business as getting." He's done plenty of both. "You can do so much damage," he says. "Make certain that you feel very good about the gifts you make. They are as important as any business investment you will make."

The rule in philanthropy, as in medicine, should be, "First, do no harm."

*T*o know even one life has breathed
easier because you have lived—
this is to have succeeded.

—Ralph Waldo Emerson

It's a great loss when you allow former board members to escape. When some of your best rotate off because of their term limitation, stay in touch.

Never let an opportunity pass without letting them know that you value their relationship. And appreciate all they have done in the past.

Look for reasons to call them and ask for counsel and advice. And, obviously, keep them on your mailing list.

You'll be going back to them. Perhaps to serve on the board again, but certainly for gifts to capital and ongoing programs.

Our colleagues in direct mail tell us that you shouldn't be afraid to ask too often. The experts tell us that it's awfully difficult to get the kind of response you need from a donor file if you are not asking them to give at least five or six times a year.

Are they offended by that many requests? No . . . they give!

There are times it can be tough. That's the truth of it. But fundraising is also exhilarating. It takes passion, commitment, and a certain degree of boldness. I sometimes compare it to **whitewater rafting**:

1. Whitewater (fundraising)—that's what you came for. Have fun and enjoy it.

2. Rest at all of the calm places—there will be more whitewater soon, perhaps more turbulent and difficult than you've been through.

3. Never stop paddling, even when it seems hopeless.

4. If you get into trouble, do not panic.

5. If you go under, remain calm and hold on to your paddle. Eventually you'll come back up.

Give your board meetings a grade. I recommend to my clients that they preassign a director, who will be the last item on the agenda. His or her role is to recap the meeting and give a verbal evaluation of special action that was taken and the issues that were discussed, and an appraisal of how valuable the meeting was to both the institution and the directors.

What happens? Well . . . something unusual. Try it a couple of times and you'll find it motivates you and the chair to have a more vital and productive meeting. It's also a great way of summing up for board members their value to the organization.

What's in a name? The going rate at New York University is rising. It is at other universities, also. You can name the new Medical School at NYU for $100 million. Or a clinical research facility for $50 million. Or go for the Department of Medicine for $20 million. But if that's too much, you can name a chair in their new auditorium for $1500.

At most of the major universities today, you can endow a chair for $1.5 million to $2 million.

Wit, Wisdom & Moxie

Everyone said it couldn't be done,
And if I tried, I'd rue it.
But I tackled the thing that couldn't be
*   done—*
And with hard work found I could do it.

How good do you look to potential endowment donors?

Studies of the generous affluent show that when they make gifts to create or advance endowment funds, your organization's ability to manage money is as important as your mission. They want to see their endowment funds grow.

One large brokerage firm actually found that many of their wealthy clients resisted endowment appeals—not because they don't like endowment funds but because they felt charities just didn't do a good job of managing money!

Donors may be onto something. A majority of endowment funds struggle to provide a steady five percent return that can be used for charitable purposes. As in many other areas, you must look beyond generally accepted orthodoxy to differentiate your organization when it comes to endowment giving and investing.

*E*nlightened givers feel the rapture of being alive.

Go ahead, make the appointment. Clear your desk and your mind of everything else. Don't let unimportant emergencies get in the way. Do it now. Make the call, get the appointment, ask for the gift.

How is it possible that you're harried and overworked, and spending ten hours a day at the office, and still making so few appointments? What are you doing instead? Organizing your desk? Attending staff meetings? Playing with e-mail and the Internet? Some will do anything to keep from picking up the phone and connecting with a prospect. Go ahead. Do it.

In most campaigns, we work with a strong mixture of the Boomers and the so-called younger generation. We find that the younger folks are every bit as interested in profit-making as their parents. But they demand another kind of return as well: emotional, spiritual, and moral. They talk plenty about mission and value—and about their profit and loss in the same breath. They want to do it all—rake it in and give it back. It's compassionate capitalism, and we see it all the time in our programs.

*E*very problem is an inspiring opportunity when pursued with a vigorous belief in the possible. An obstacle is something you see when you take your eyes off the important objective. Great and exciting opportunity stands before you every moment.

Donors demand fiscal responsibility. Those who give to you want to know that you are using their funds wisely and putting their money to proper and effective use. They want to make certain that their funds are achieving the anticipated objectives.

A whopping nine out of ten donors rate financial accountability as one of the most important factors in determining their gift. Because it's so important, you need to talk about it and write about your concern for accountability, your sense of responsibility, and your focus on financial stewardship in all of your material. Accountability counts.

I like the idea that supervisors conduct job performance reviews every three months, and comprehensive assessments every year. It's the best way to keep problems from recurring. It's also a superb way for the supervisor to show appreciation for a job well done. Doing reviews quarterly ensures that employees know where they stand and how the supervisor feels about their performance.

Regular reviews allow for short- and long-term objective-setting—and re-setting, if necessary.

*N*ever believe that a few caring people can't change the world. For,
indeed, that's all who ever have.

—Margaret Mead

Time . . . your most precious asset, and your worst enemy! If you find that you don't have enough time to get everything else done, you're not alone. But there is a way to take a more decisive hold on your life and job.

To start, examine your calendar. If most appointments are unrelated to your primary responsibility and the institution's vision for the future, you're probably spending time on what's unessential. Consider these dispensables as traitors and criminals to your cause!

Concentrate on the imperatives of your job. Nothing else counts.

Creative recognition and genuine appreciation, repeated appropriately, become the first step in getting the next gift. The receipt and the letter of acknowledgment set the stage for the next gift—a larger one! This mustn't be hit or miss. Develop a written and specific plan.

*P*rocrastination is your mortal enemy. The avenue of despair and disappointment is lined with the timid and tired who don't get things done, who won't act. These men and women conspire with the devil of failure. You must embrace the day, ravish the moment, wring and wrest from it all that is good, and it will yield.

At one of your staff meetings, discuss what is unique about your organization. Spend the time necessary for a thorough discussion. Don't worry if the list becomes long.

Then, with a group, begin honing the list until you come up with three or four areas where you feel you are truly different and uncommon compared to other organizations, particularly those in competition with you.

Keep hammering away at this. People give because they believe in the mission of your institution and your uniqueness. From this will grow the passion and commitment. If you're simply a carbon copy of another organization—why should anyone care?

I just read a study the other day. In it, respondents claim that the most important factors in deciding which charities to support are the institution's reputation and integrity (80 percent), the needs being met by the institution (79 percent), and the charity's effectiveness in using funds (75 percent).

I have never settled for better, when best was within reach. I have no tolerance or interest in "okay" or "good enough." I've never mistaken hearing for listening.

I've been difficult when necessary. I've been easy when faced with perfection. I spend my life lighting fires.

I know that integrity and values are not the best policy. They are the only policy.

I believe in miracles. I know that to say "impossible" always puts you on the losing side.

I love big, bold audacious dreams. There's magic in them. They make non-believers stand on tip-toes.

For me, this profession has been a ministry. I know that's perhaps a bit "heavy" for some. But I know of no other way of putting it. A ministry! That's it. And every step along the path, a joyful journey filled with new challenges, opportunities unending, and a passion that burns in my bones.

One of the basic verities of our work is: It is harder to get an appointment than it is to get the gift. Once you have the appointment, you're 85 percent of the way toward getting the gift.

Send a letter first. That's often the best way to break the ice. But it has to come from someone who knows the prospect well . . . and has some leverage. The letter lets you avoid making a cold call.

Be prepared. And practice. Practice. Know what to say—and how to say it—to make the appointment. Be certain to have your calendar handy. **Remember:** Your job is not to make the case or discuss the gift. Your objective is to line up the appointment.

See the Appendix for a sample of a pre-call letter that really works.

Making the Ask

A tired and haggard fundraiser
Met the Devil at Hell's gate.
"What have you done," asked Satan,
"To earn this terrible fate?"

"I don't know," the fundraiser said,
"I never shirked a duty or a task.
I called on every prospect . . . but
I guess I failed to make the ask."

The Devil showed no mercy,
With disgust he rang the bell.
"I condemn you to an eternity," he said
"In the fires of the deepest hell."

This I
Believe . . .

Stop for a moment.

I want you to think about what passions drive your life. What do you stand for? What are the principles that temper the spirit and heart of your character and being?

I "discovered" my beliefs when I decided one day to put them into writing. A credo of sorts.

After I completed it, I gave a copy to each staff member of our firm. I was so delighted to discover who I was, I wanted them to know the kind of person they were working with—the strengths and . . . and, yes, the weaknesses. I wanted them to know of my expectations for them. I thought we would work much more effectively if they understood me better. The good and the bad.

And, now, I want to share my list with you. You may not agree with any of it. I won't be surprised if you don't. But remember—it's my code of conduct, not yours!

When I finished my list, I thought it was one of the most important exercises I had undertaken—because, suddenly, I got to know myself.

I strongly suggest that you prepare a list of your own beliefs. Go ahead, do it! It can be frightening. (Mine was, in some ways.) But it will also be revealing. I discovered who I was.

251

Wit, Wisdom & Moxie

"This I believe . . ."—the signposts on my life's journey:

The Highest Quality. My foremost and overriding objective for the firm is to make it the best and most highly esteemed in the nation. I want us to have a reputation and a practice for being a firm of high quality and standards, superb service to clients, creativity, style, and flair. The goals of all staff members—no matter what their position—should be compatible with these.

Communicate. One of the primary jobs of the staff is to keep me out of trouble! The way you achieve this is to make certain that you are providing high-level service and effective performance in all you do. You also keep me out of trouble by keeping me fully informed. I do a pretty good job of staying in contact, but it's your responsibility to be certain I know what is happening in your area of work.

Be Certain to Ask. It is your responsibility to understand fully the firm's philosophy of operation and the factors that relate to your job and govern how you succeed. If anything of significance is unclear, you have a responsibility to ask questions.

Remembering. Through whatever method you find successful, you must remember items of importance and those requiring some sort of action. Find a technique that works for you, whatever it is. I give high marks to staff members who have a good memory. And it's an attribute that can be learned and acquired. If you don't have a good memory, find a system that works for you. And use it.

Responding. I am compulsive about writing memos, perhaps to a fault. In many of these memos, I ask for a response or an evaluation. I expect this to be done as quickly and thoroughly as possible. I get upset when I ask for a response and don't receive one.

Overtime. It is the nature of our service that it is often necessary to work long hours. This is not necessarily desirable, but on the other hand, it is not unusual in other professions. Overtime and long hours seem to be essential because that's what it takes to get a particular job done—on time, with effectiveness, and a high level of quality. I believe firmly that it's important to work hard, work long, and work joyously.

Your Health and Vitality. You are expected to maintain a desirable level of physical fitness. This will enable you to function at full mental capacity and at a proper level of zeal for the work. We are judged by the way we act and look. You should be perceived as vital, vigorous, and charged with energy. Through good physical conditioning, you can maintain a proper attitude that will help you cope with stress and a demanding job. I'm a great advocate of vitamins, exercise, and positive mental attitude. Anyone who considers this mumbo-jumbo will have a difficult time dealing with me! *Snap, crackle, pop*—that's what I expect. I demand it from myself and hope for it from all on our staff.

Your Problems. I shall try to be sensitive and anticipate your problems. But don't make me guess or allow something to go on that is unknown to me. It is your responsibility to tell me about concerns and problems that you have—personal and professional.

Innovation. I believe that creativity is of great significance in our work and that our firm should reward innovation in our staff. We are known nationally as being one of the most creative firms in the business. This is a battle that is not ever finally won, but must be waged day after day. I believe that the staff must eschew everything that is dull, motionless, backward-looking. It must seek new ways, new solutions. A staff and a firm that is serving today as it did yesterday, is bound to lose. A firm and staff that serves tomorrow as it does today . . . is doomed.

Appearance. How you dress and your appearance is important because it creates an image of the firm for everyone we contact. I consider appropriate dress to be essential. The firm is often judged, rightly or wrongly, on your presence and appearance. I agree with most authorities on proper attire that anything that calls undue attention to your dress or appearance is inappropriate.

The Will to Win. I don't suffer failure easily. And I'm not really pleased with a staff person who does—not anyone, not in anything. That doesn't mean that we compromise our integrity or principles in any way in order to win—it's just that I can't remember undertaking anything in life when I didn't set out to win. I follow the principle of: "Show me a good loser . . . and I'll show you a loser."

Do What You Say. Don't make promises you can't keep. I don't, and I don't expect the staff to. If you say you're going to do something, do it. And if I tell you I am going to do something, you should expect it to be done. That's a commitment I make to you and to our clients.

Surprises Are Bad. I am in the same league with everyone else in this regard. I don't like to be surprised. It is your responsibility to keep me fully informed.

Errors of Commission. I prefer errors of commission to errors of omission. Often, it is better to do something, even if it is wrong. You'll find that I shall often talk with you about things that I consider to be a mistake or not in keeping with the operation of the firm—but I shall always support you. If you do something and it is wrong, we can probably correct it. But we can't correct a nothing! However, I don't like to correct something more than once.

Have Fun. I agree with Auntie Mame: *Life should be a glorious feast . . . but some poor souls are starving to death.* I think your work should be fun, a great joy. If it is, you'll show it in everything you do—and your zest will be contagious. If you're not having fun, that will show, also. You have a right to expect work that's enjoyable and fun. If it isn't, we should talk.

Clients Come First. In almost every single decision I make, I consider first and primary the impact it will have on our clients. The client is foremost in my thoughts and in the expenditure of my energy. I find it intolerable if we have not served a client properly. It is the one area where it is most difficult for me to support our staff. I am the most unforgiving of myself in this regard. I am committed to premier service and want our staff to have the same standards.

Your Objectives. You are expected to develop measurable objectives for the areas of your responsibility. You are expected to indicate how you hope to change, improve, and meet new and demanding objectives. Without these plans, you are drifting like a ship without a rudder.

Punctuality. You are expected to be punctual to all meetings and commitments. Time is a precious commodity for everyone and keeping others waiting is rude. Being punctual is only a matter of habit.

Loyalty. You are expected to support decisions made by your supervisors. That doesn't necessarily mean a blind loyalty or that your shouldn't challenge or question. Let us know your opinion. But once the decision is made, it is not to be criticized publicly to peers, subordinates, or clients. My feeling is that if you feel you cannot be loyal, you should seek other employment. I shall help you find a new position.

Enthusiasm. The words come from two Greek words. **En** means "in" or "within." And **theos** means "God." That's it! To have enthusiasm is to have God within us. The Greeks used the term to mean: To be in a state of being inspired by God. By nature, I'm enthusiastic. Some would say I'm a roaring enthusiast! I do seem to have a gusto for what I do and for life. And I like to be around staff who exhibit this same kind of fervor and passion. It's infectious.

What Comes First. Morals. Ethics. Standards. Integrity. For the firm and for each staff member. Deeds not words. For us, integrity isn't the best policy—it is the only policy. It can be a rigorous test. For a staff member and the firm, integrity isn't a sometime thing. It is everything.

Optimism and Positive Attitude. For some, it is easy to find the negative and the gray in every situation and in every person. However, I look for and expect a staff that is positive in its attitude, even under the most trying of conditions. Your positive attitude is infectious for everyone. Devote your energy to developing yourself and all others in the organization. Don't tear down. Don't be negative. Be a builder. Seek the bright side, the positive.

The Firm's Goals. I believe in audacious objectives. I feel it's important for the firm and to the staff to have to stand on tip-toes, to reach high, to keep raising the bar. For our firm, in all we do, I seek four overriding objectives: to be the best, do the most, get there first . . . and to make a difference. I believe in dazzling dreams and glorious visions. I seek colleagues who share these objectives with the same passion I have.

A Can-Do Attitude. I honestly believe that there isn't anything I undertake that I can't do. I really believe it—and I expect a staff that does, also. Or at the very least, tries like the dickens to achieve it. I CAN DO IT is my credo, my hymn. I really believe in it and I try to practice it. And I would like to feel that we have a staff that believes this, also. I am convinced that if you feel you can—you can. I believe in miracles. I try to "think a miracle" in everything I do. I believe that saying impossible always puts you on the losing side. For me, it's: decide, dare, do.

Hard Work. I really believe in hard work. I am fully aware that I am a person of only average skill and talent—perhaps a certain flair and style, and some intelligence. I recall that when I was quite young it occurred to me that most people are willing to work seven or eight hours a day. But I believed that if I worked 12 or 14 hours—I would have an extra half day on those other folks every day. I don't feel that's right for everyone. I'm not certain that it's even right for me or my family. But I'm too old to change. I do like a staff with the same work ethic. I know full well that admonition: "Work smarter, not harder." But I have also found that the harder you work, the smarter and luckier you get.

Do It Now. TNT—Today, Not Tomorrow. That's the hymn I sing. *Carpe Diem* is a Latin phrase which means; Seize the day, seize the moment. Ah, that's my creed. I rejoice in the present because I know the day is aglow with towering opportunities.

The Box
Is Not Full

Dear **Reader:** I want to send you a gift. Something very special.

Think of a box. A big wooden box. Let's say something as large as your refrigerator. Close your eyes for a moment and picture it.

You ask: "What's the box for?"

To put notes in.

"What kind of notes?"

Messages for you. Special notes and bits and pieces, tiny memos. And the kind thoughts and fond wishes I want to send you. That's what's in the box.

Nearly everything I could think of is in it. But still the box is not full. So I included some notes for happiness and joy. And good health, too. Wishes for never-ending

257

fulfillment. And a heart of grace, compassion, and an understanding spirit.

And still the box is not full.

I added high hopes and lofty expectations. And messages for noble objectives, success, and achievement. Then I put in the warm thoughts I have for you and how much you mean to me.

Still, the box is not quite full.

And then I added all the love and gratitude I feel for you.

Appendix

The No Nonsense Guide
to Help You Prepare
a Statement of Your Case

"This draft of the Case Statement has my basic thrust. Have it fleshed out, pretty'd up, fussed over, given a shot of pizzazz, minimize the cost of the project, make the memorial opportunities sexier, shorten the headlines but add a lot more sizzle, get more exciting photos, cut the length, give me more details, find more inspiring quotations, get Board approval, and have it back tomorrow morning in final form."

YOUR VISION

Men and women will give sacrificially of their time, talents, and funds— if they believe in the value and integrity of your services and programs. A devotion to the mission of your institution leads to commitment and dedication. And that leads to dollars. You can count on it! There is no other factor as important. Nothing else even comes close.

Every organization and institution needs a basic document that sets forth its nature, purpose, and principal objectives. That document is often called a Case Statement. In business and corporate parlance, it is referred to as The Prospectus. Your major donors and leaders will understand that term. In our firm, we most often call it a Vision Statement— because we feel that there is nothing that has more dramatic and powerful impact than the proper interpretation of your dreams and your visions for the future. That is the magic!

The Case should state the type and scope of service you now provide and your objectives for the future. Here are some important components of a typical statement:

- Why are your activities and programs important

- Who benefits

- What is your philosophy of operation and your mission— your Grand Design

- What opportunities do you seek for greater service

- What is the nature and extent of your financial needs

- In what ways will you become a stronger and more effective organization

- How will the funds you seek help your institution serve more effectively and fulfill your mission

- What imperatives propel and move your organization forward

- Why are you worthy of voluntary effort and support

For a capital or endowment campaign, the Vision Statement is of critical significance. It is essential. It is everything.

But whether you are planning a major fundraising effort or not, you should have a Vision Statement that is current. And it should be reviewed, assessed, and revised on a regular basis. It is your basic document— that which gives spirit, vitality, and purpose to all you do. It is your Institutional Credo.

261

IF A SIXTH GRADER CAN UNDERSTAND IT, YOU'RE ON THE RIGHT TRACK

A t the heart of your Case Statement, there must be a description of your objective and institutional purpose— your very special mission. It describes the philosophy and focus of your operation which makes you invincible! It is the platform which launches your program, and gives heart and character to the service you provide. The Mission Statement is not a sloganism— it is the life of your organization. Here are six points which will be of help.

1 The statement of your mission is an enabling and empowering document. It is the engine which powers your institutional train. It uniquely combines your ethos, rationale, and philosophy— that memorializes and at the same time places into action your uncompromising purpose.

Putting into precise words this institutional covenant can be fiercely awesome— and requires deep introspection, careful scrutiny, and clear expression. It becomes your conscience and your guide. It is the overriding criterion by which you monitor and measure the health of your organization. It provides direction, determination, and dedication to all programs and services you offer.

2 The Mission Statement needs to describe how your organization chooses to bring about change. It is not described in terms of the programs and objectives necessary to achieve change. It is the change itself that becomes your mission.

3 The clutter and clang of an overly long Mission Statement makes it impossible to find the special core of the Statement itself. Keep it brief. Hone the words until there isn't any fat left.

4 The Statement should be understandable. If a sixth grade student can read, comprehend, and explain the Statement— you are probably on the right track.

5 The Statement should be reviewed, discussed, and approved by the Board of Directors. And then it should be assessed on a regular basis to make certain that both your institution and the Mission continue to be relevant and in concert, one with the other.

6 Once the Mission is approved, it must become the organization's credo, its anthem, the hymn it continually sings— with gusto, conviction, and zeal.

SEVEN WAYS A CASE STATEMENT IS USED

A carefully conceived, well-developed statement of your vision and need will assure that you:

1 Secure agreement, understanding, and commitment among your primary leaders and Board members— so that there is total dedication to the cause and a precise focus of the institution's objectives and long-range goals.

2 Have a direction and a defined strategy for how to most effectively present your vision and your case to your primary constituencies.

3 Inform leaders and workers of your program and your dreams— and demonstrate how the success of the endeavor will work to the immense benefit of those you serve.

4 Enlist new leaders to your cause— in sufficient numbers and at the proper level to win the effort.

5 Have an early working document and cultivation piece for prospective major donors.

6 Have a document that helps others endorse and share your vision— and accept greater and ever-expanding responsibility of identifying with your invincible mission and dreams.

7 Have a source book and guide for the writing of subsequent publications, articles, foundation proposals, and videotaped presentations.

SPEAK VERY SOFTLY.
IT WILL SOUND LIKE THUNDER

T he typical statement runs from 10 to 30 pages of double-spaced manuscript. But don't worry about how long or short it is. It needs to be as long as it needs to be! And no longer. A prospect will read a long document if it is well written. And a short statement not well written— will not be read at all. Don't worry about the pages. Worry about the writing.

The case is seldom a printed piece. It certainly should not look slick or expensive. More commonly, it is typed and photocopied and used for limited distribution.

The rationale for such a format is to avoid a piece that looks costly. That is often a turn-off. Desktop publishing, however, has increased the possibilities for cost-effective type-setting, design, and printing.

Here are some other tips:

- The Vision Statement is most often not a signed article, although it occasionally appears as a statement of the governing board of the institution.

- There are times when an introductory letter, signed by the chief volunteer officer, establishes the appropriate tone and setting.

- It need not be illustrated— but photographs, graphs, maps, or charts can be very effective and compelling in making the case.

- Emotion outpulls intellect every time. Go for the visceral. But it has to be believable.

- Statistics don't have sizzle! You've heard the story about the one fellow who says to the other: "A person is hit by a car every 18 seconds." The other fellow says: "That guy must be pretty bruised up at the end of the day." But if the statistics are dramatic and demonstrate sizable growth or need, they can often be displayed dramatically in a graph. Better still, instead of statistics, use actual cases, real stories, and write about victims or success stories. That will bring vital life (and dollars) to dull statistics.

- Often individual copies are numbered and registered. That helps give the feeling of "a limited edition to select friends."

- Methods of binding vary, but should seldom be elaborate. You may find that a three-ring binder is most effective. No one throws away a three-ring binder!

- Make it comprehensive— but not superfluous. And that's a fine line.

- And never forget . . . the thundering and dramatic impact of the understated.

THE NINE ESSENTIALS YOU HAVE TO COVER

There are nine areas you will need to describe and interpret. They almost always comprise the subject matter of the case. They need not necessarily follow in the order shown below.

The History of the Organization. This will be particularly important if your roots are deep and your heritage rich. Why and how did you come into existence? What issues caused your formation? Describe the social and demographic setting. Describe in dramatic terms your incomparable mission. But keep this all brief. Remember you are making the case for your future and your dreams-not your distinguished past!

The Problem and the Opportunity. A statement of the social problem which creates the need for the particular project or program. Describe the compelling opportunity and challenge for service that is presented to your institution at this time. Write about the urgency. Keep in mind that people are most persuasively motivated by what saves lives or changes lives. Do not describe how the proposed program will help the institution— about how it will help people. It is important that the case has a larger platform than the institution itself.

Proposed Solution. The institution's plan for solving the problem and why it seeks this particular opportunity for greater services.

The Institution's Unique Role. Why your particular institution is best qualified to respond to the problem, meet the challenge, render the proposed service.

The Goals. A description and the justification of fundraising projects.

The Fundraising Equation. In the financing of the proposed plan, who should be responsible? What are the sources of funding that will combine to make the goal? What part does private philanthropy play in that equation?

The Fundraising Plan. How you propose to raise the required funds and any evidence that this plan will be successful.

How to Give. Statements concerning the nature and kind of gifts you seek.

Leadership. The names and qualifications of those who will lead the fundraising program, as well as those who will be ultimately responsible for the program and policies for spending the money.

Wit, Wisdom & Moxie

USE A TEAM APPROACH.
IT ASSURES SUCCESS.

A statement of its case is probably the single most important document that an institution ever prepares. The best talents and most responsible authorities of the organization should be involved in its production.

It may be developed and written by the staff, although it is much more effective to have the staff and Board work in concert in the preparation. Finally, it should be approved by the Board. This assures all are in agreement and understand fully the thrust and forward focus of the organization.

Truly effective and memorable case statements are seldom produced exclusively by an outside writer without the intimate and whole-hearted cooperation of those who know the institution best. And for a variety of reasons, the best statements are not often produced internally by the institution's staff.

The most formidable Vision Statements are probably produced by a four-step process:

- Those who are best informed about the institution furnish the data and basic material.

- A skilled professional writer— who understands fundraising and the preparation of statements— develops the information, determines the concept, and puts the material in written form.

- The organization then edits the statement so that "it sounds like us."

- The professional writer then redrafts the statement to incorporate the organization's changes and suggestions.

What is too often overlooked in this process is its value in unifying the opinions of the leaders of the organization. The preparation of a case can be wonderfully effective in clarifying vague understandings, securing agreement on fundamental principles, and focusing everyone's thinking on the real issues confronting the institution.

Unless they are experienced in fundraising, few writers— no matter how talented— can prepare an effective statement. And almost never— an advertising or public relations firm.

Developing a Vision Statement is a milestone in the life of an organization. Because of the importance of the process and the experience, we recommend that responsibility for it be retained by the governing board itself, or by a high level committee, with proper staff support and technical assistance. Keep in mind, however, that it is said that a camel started off as a horse that was reviewed by a committee! Limit the number of people who are granted editing privileges.

"A man who knows not how to write may think this is no great feat. But only try to do it yourself and you will learn how arduous is the writer's task. It dims your eyes, makes your back ache, and knits your chest and belly together— it is a terrible ordeal for the human body.

So, gentle reader, turn these pages carefully and keep your fingers far from the text."

Prior Robert Alden
c 1300 AD

EVEN THE BEST WRITER CAN'T OVERCOME
A WEAK INSTITUTION

A tiger chatted with a lion— as they drank by the side of a pool. "Tell me," said the tiger, "why you're always roaring like a fool."

"It's not so foolish," said the lion with a twinkle in his eye. "They call me King of Beasts, which proves it pays to advertise."

A little rabbit overheard this conversation and he raced home like a streak. He thought he'd try the lion's plan— but his roar was just a squeek.

And a hungry fox that morning had his breakfast in the woods. Which only goes to prove— It doesn't pay to advertise when you haven't got the goods.

No matter how skillful and creative the writer is, you cannot conceal an institutional lack of a well-defined and important purpose. No matter how compelling the copy, you cannot fabricate a dedication to significant and attainable goals. The organization must have the capacity and credibility to justify to the donor that his or her dollars will be used wisely and effectively— a happy mixture of institutional experience, capable staff and volunteer management, and proven efficiency and success. No mumbo jumbo. No flim-flam.

The writing of a case is not so much an experience in creativity, as an expression in self-revelation. A mediocre or unworthy institution cannot produce or substantiate a great case.

To prepare a carefully documented case— a statement that propels and motivates one to action— requires an appropriate amount of time. Don't push it! But if it takes too long, something is wrong. It probably means that some of the pieces are missing. Or you don't have a truly valid case. Or you have the wrong writer.

Too many case statements are merely self-adulation. But the case is not for the purpose of praising the institution. It is for heralding the institution's ethos— its purpose and objectives. It must motivate the reader to identify with that purpose and those objectives.

A really powerful case will be more concerned with the cause that the institution represents and the problem it seeks to resolve— than with the institution itself. Not easily achieved, this subtle approach!

If your institution has the will and the faith— you can break all barriers, overcome any obstacles, and achieve great things.

WATCH OUT FOR THE SIX PITFALLS.
THEY'LL BURY YOU.

1 **Undefined Purpose.** The reasons your organization exists should be described in compelling terms. A clear statement of your mission and your vision is perhaps the central function of the case.

2 **Overstated Emotionalism.** It is perhaps natural and understandable to try to convey in writing how those who are closest to the organization feel about it. This sort of case may work with the most loyal alums of a college or the most grateful patients of a hospital— but is not always the most effective approach for those outside the inner circle. Keep in mind the powerful impact of the understated.

3 **The Pleading of Needs.** The fact that an institution has large and urgent financial needs is not a good reason for the dispassionate reader to make a gift. Every institution has needs. The reader is persuaded and moved by exhilarating opportunities— the promise of effective action and the solution to human and social problems. Dwelling on financial problems may, in fact, cause the potential donor to question the institution's financial management and stability. It may sound like a bad investment. Remember: Gifts come to institutions with answers and solutions not to those with financial problems and needs.

"Who the devil wrote this terrible Case Statement. It comes perilously close to the truth!"

4 **Misunderstanding What Motivates a Prospect.** Volunteer leaders and prospective donors are most often interested in the financial stability of the institution, the cost of the proposed project, and how the completed program will be funded in future years. Sure— they're interested in the cause and the project. But they also want to see the bottom line. They want to know about your past— in relation to your present and your future. They want to know how it will make their community a better place in which to live and do business. A too-lengthy history or a massive missile in which the facts are difficult to find can drown the reader. The quality of a statement is not to be measured in sheer weight!

5 **Vague Plans.** Planning should be fairly well completed before the case statement is issued. Vague and uncertain plans do not inspire.

6 **Unsubstantiated Grand Claims.** It is easy— and tempting to engage in chestbeating. Claims to eternal and infinite significance must be supported by commensurate documentation. Darn!

THE WRITE STUFF

Each writer has a style uniquely his own. (Okay, okay— you prefer. . . "a style uniquely his or her own!") But we'd like to suggest a few things to keep in mind to help you create a document with a sense of force and urgency.

Sell Your Reader. Don't lean over backwards to present your facts too objectively. Sure, tell the truth— but you must state your case in a manner that propels the reader to get out the checkbook. You must sell. And you must ask for the order.

Appeal First to the Emotions— Then to the Intellect. Personalize statistics with true stories and case studies. Resist the mundane. Talk about a specific heart patient or a girl that turned her life around with the scholarship she received. Describe a child with cerebral palsy who takes his first step. Tell the story of Johnny, a delinquent, whose life was changed by the Boys Club. Don't be subtle, be specific, use names— and if it makes the reader tingle and break out in goose bumps . . . well, you're on your way to a gift!

Hone Your Words Painstakingly. Some words are more positive, more powerful than others. When you are talking about the project, say what wonderful things it will (not "would") make possible. Never ask for help. Instead, talk in terms of the opportunity the campaign presents to the donor. Focus on the incredible work that is accomplished in a less than adequate facility, rather than describing a place so squalid and unsafe that the organization couldn't possibly be doing a decent job. Do you remember how much fun it was to get a gift at Christmas or on a birthday? A gift is fun, with very positive connotations. A pledge, a contribution, even a donation— these don't have the same warm-fuzzies as the magic word: Gift.

Break the Copy with Interesting Headings and Sub-Heads. Give readers a chance to pause and catch their breath.

"I'm willing to give to you if I'm properly motivated by a Case Statement that has high dramatic and emotional impact."

Tell Your Readers What You Want Them To Do. If your case is being used for a feasibility study, say that the institution welcomes the interviewee's ideas and involvement. If the case is used as the principal campaign publication, ask specifically, for a generous gift.

Be Certain to Use Visual Aids and Quotations. Maps, graphs, photographs, and charts add high impact to the case. Use quotations from the institution's "users," well-known citizens in the community who endorse the project and the institution, and others who can speak to the need for the project in the community. Or try a famous author, an artist, philosopher, or an expert in the institution's field of service. This will underline your message and add credibility.

Remember, the Vision Statement should move the reader to action. If it is sufficiently dramatic and appealing, the case transforms the institution into a cause. And causes are what motivate men and women to action.

THE FAIL-PROOF CHECKLIST

Here are some questions to ask, examine . . . and then answer, in preparing material for your Vision Statement. You can have total confidence in this list nothing has been forgotten. Use it as a guide to compliment the other areas indicated throughout this document. Check off each question as you complete the material.

√	How Is The Institution Positioned In The Community And What Is Its Heritage?
	When was the institution founded?
	What were the circumstances surrounding the beginnings?
	What geographical area does the institution serve?
	Natural resources in the area?
	Industrial and business concentration?
	What distinguishes the area from the rest of the country, state, or nation— a capital, a distribution center, a rural area?
	Describe the population of the service area.
	Population trends. Increasing or decreasing? Aging?
	Level of affluence and occupational types.
	Educational level and cultural types.
	Ethnic origins.

√	How Does The Institution Benefit The Community— How And Who Does It Serve?
	What are the services offered by the institution?
	How many people use these services? Have they been increased or decreased? Why?
	How much do each of these services cost? Are they furnished free or subsidized?
	What are the services offered by other organizations in the institution's service area?
	Is there any duplication of services or is the organization's niche unique?
	Does the institution cooperate with other organizations in joining programs or use of facilities?
	In the community, is there a need for services not currently being met that the institution could fill if it had increased funds?
	How many potential new users of the institution could you expect to attract if its programs were increased?

√	Why Is A Fundraising Program Necessary?
	Why does the institution need funds?
	Is the program for capital or endowment or both?
	Specific components of the campaign and project?
	How will the campaign improve the organization's ability to fulfill its mission?
	How much money does the institution need?
	How will the money be raised?
	Have alternative sources of funding been investigated? (government grants, bonds, etc.)

√	Is The Institution Fiscally Sound?
	What is the current operating budget?
	Is the institution operating in the black?
	Who makes the major contribution to the present operating budget?
	Does the institution have a membership drive, annual support campaign, admission fee, or subscriptions?
	Does it have an endowment?
	What are the financial assets and liabilities of the institution?
	Are the fees charged (if any) competitive?
	Does the institution have a Planned Giving program?

√	Does The Institution Have Strong Leadership?
	What is the composition of the Board of Directors (or Trustees)?
	How many are on the Board?
	Are different ages and both sexes represented?
	Major business and commercial interests?
	Community minorities or institution's constituency?
	Is the staff well qualified?
	How many persons are on the staff?
	What are the major strengths and accomplishments of the Executive Director and other key staff?
	Does the institution use volunteers and are they effective?
	Do the administrative facilities meet the requirements of the staff and volunteers?

Time Allocation
and Priorities

This won't be easy! You are being asked to analyze as closely as possible how you spend your time. Not your hours . . . but how you allocate your time, on a percentage basis, to the necessary functions of your work. Don't worry about being precise—what is important is that there be a general indication of your work day. Think of a typical week or month. And, yes, we know—there's nothing typical about your work. Not ever! But do the best you can. And if the totals come to a lot more than one hundred percent—something's wrong! Rework the TAP. Then, after you have completed the first column, indicate in the second column what you feel is a desirable allocation of your time if you are to be your most effective best and perform at optimum efficiency.

Functions	% Actual	% Desirable
Meetings with Supervisors		
Staff Meetings		
Meetings with Individual Staff Members		
Administration, Management, and Supervision		
Involvement in Corporate Institutional Affairs		
New Donor Prospect Identification		
New Donor Prospect Contacts		
Donor Contacts and Cultivation		
Actual Solicitation for Gifts		
Identification and Prospecting for New Board Members		
Individual Meetings with Board and Committee Members		
Meetings of the Board and Committees		
Community Activities		
Initiating and Returning Telephone Calls		
Paperwork, Reviewing Mail, Work at Desk		
Writing Letters, Memos, etc.		
Professional Reading		
Professional Meetings and Travel		
Other		

Contacts
Grid

Performance Goals for Major Gift and Planned Giving Officers							
Standard	Total Calls Per Week	# Cold Calls Per Week	# Cultivation Calls Per Week	# Stewardship Calls Per Week	Asks Made or Proposals Delivered Per Month	Gifts Secured Per Month	Dollars Secured Per Year
Excellent	10–15	2–3	5–10	no less than 1 or more than 2	7–10	6	$1 Million
Average	7–9	2	3–5	no less than 1 or more than 3	4–6	5	$750,000
Minimum	5–6	1	2–3	no less than 1 or more than 4	2–5	3	$500,000

- The Major/Planned Gifts officer should be:
  - acquainted with 400 to 500 people
  - able to handle 100 to 150 prospects, including donor stewardship and maintenance
  - able to manage 50 to 75 prospects with 7 to 10 MOVES per year
- A call is consciousness penetration with the prospect regarding your organization. A move is a planned contact with a fixed action and objective. It may be accomplished by letter, telephone, or personal visit. The target with good prospects should be one call (MOVE) per month (12 per year) with at least 4 to 5 of those in the form of a personal visit.
- Stewardship calls are essential, but must not take the place of prospecting and gift enhancement. That is why they receive diminishing priority in these standards.

Sample Statement of Understanding

STATEMENT OF UNDERSTANDING
FOR MEMBERS OF THE BOARD OF DIRECTORS
MT. ANYWHERE FOUNDATION

As a member of the Board of Directors of the Foundation, I am fully committed to the vision and service of Mt. Anywhere and am dedicated to carrying out its mission and the work of the Foundation. I understand that in accepting this position on the Foundation Board:

1 I am responsible, with other board members, for friendraising and fundraising for Mt. Anywhere. I will take an active part in reviewing, approving, monitoring, and achieving our objectives.

2 I take a responsibility in knowing as much as I can about the Medical Center, its work and outreach, and its vision for the future.

3 I accept the mission of Mt. Anywhere and understand that through my efforts, I contribute to the health and vitality of its service and work.

4 I will give what is for me as substantial a financial donation as possible. I may give this as a one-time donation each year, or I may commit to give a certain amount several times during the year.

5 I understand that as a board member, I lead the way. I am a model for others to follow. If I, as a board member, do not care enough to work and give, why should anyone else?

6 I will actively engage in fundraising in whatever ways are best suited for me and most effectively serve the purposes of Mt. Anywhere. This may include individual solicitation, involvement in special events, writing mail appeals, and the like. I am willing to make a good-faith agreement to do my best and to raise as much money as I can.

7 I will be an enthusiastic booster, a positive advocate for Mt. Anywhere.

8 I will attend board meetings, be available for phone consultation, and serve on at least one committee. If I am not able to meet my obligations as a board member, I understand that I may be asked to offer my resignation.

9 I will do all I can to support the staff, and encourage them to grow professionally and personally. I will be prepared to assist them whenever it is appropriate. I also understand that there are times I must stay out of their way! I won't manage— but I will encourage and expect the best results possible, the highest quality work possible, and ever-increasing production. Working together with the staff, we can achieve high objectives.

10   I will bring the *Six As* to my Foundation Board tenure. I will:

> *be an* **Ambassador**
> *be an* **Advisor**
> *be an* **Advocate**
> *provide* **Access**
> *provide* **Affluence**
> *provide* **Assistance**

11   Among the boards I serve on, I shall consider my work with the Mt. Anywhere Foundation to be my most important priority— or at the very least, no lower than second in importance.

12   In signing this document, I understand that no quotas are being set, and no rigid standards of measurement and achievement are being established. Every board member makes a statement of faith to be a partner with every other board member to strive for the great success of our cause. We trust each other to carry out the above agreements to the best of our ability.

_____
Signature of Board Member

In its turn, the Mt. Anywhere Foundation is responsible to you in a number of ways. Here are some:

1   You will regularly receive status reports and information about our work, service, and progress.

2   You can call on the staff at any time to discuss programs and policies, goals, and objectives.

3   You can count on the staff to support your work in every way possible.

4   We shall do our best to make board meetings as substantive and productive as possible— with as little lost and meaningless time as possible.

5   We shall encourage you to take an increasingly larger role in leadership.

6   Board members and staff will respond to the best of their ability in a straight-forward and thorough fashion to any questions you have that you feel are necessary to carry out your responsibilities to Mt. Anywhere.

7   You can expect the staff and all board members to make this the most rewarding and fulfilling volunteer experience you have ever had.

_____   _____
Signature of the Chair   *Signature of the Executive Director*

Sample Pre-call Letter

I.M. SMART
345 Carey Street
Middleton, Ohio 97348

Dear Mary and John:

I've asked Sandra Guest to call in the next few days to set a time when we might visit you. As you well know, Sandra heads the development program for Middleton School and is a remarkable person.

I think you know how involved I've been with Middleton School. I've served on the Board for nine years— and have seen first-hand the great work they do. All of my children have gone to the school and have done wonders at College. They couldn't have had a better education than the one they received at Middleton. But you know that first-hand— your two sons are in the school now.

We're in the early stages of launching a campaign to build a new Library and add to our Endowment. It's terribly exciting. I won't bore you with the details now but when we see you, we'll discuss it in detail. I think that you'll be as excited about in the program as I am.

We're not going to ask you for money. At least not on this visit! And I made Sandra promise that she wouldn't ask for a gift either.

All we want is an opportunity to talk about the program, ask for your good counsel and advice, and determine what might be appropriate next steps. If there are not to be any next steps, that's up to you.

Thanks so much, Mary and John. I consider this a favor of the highest order. I do look forward to seeing you soon.

Sincerely,

I.M. Smart

ABOUT THE AUTHOR

When one of the supposed giants in our field complained to a friend about the shortage of really great fundraisers in the country, the friend replied: "There's probably one fewer than you think!"

I decided early on to pursue a career in fundraising. In this regard, I am unlike most in the profession. I knew from the moment I made my first call on a prospect that whatever was involved in this business, it was for me. I loved it! It embodied everything in life I cared about. I was born to raise.

That doesn't mean that I have all the qualities necessary to make a great fundraiser. Far from it. But I can tell you this: I have never stopped working at them.

We can all grow. I know this is true. We can hone our skills and talents. We can learn to climb mountains we never thought possible. This knowledge drives me on.

Someone once told me that my career has had five stages: (1) Who is Jerry Panas? (2) Get me Jerry Panas. (3) We need someone like Jerry Panas. (4) What we need is a young Jerry Panas. (5) Who is Jerry Panas?

I believe that I am somewhere between stages two and three. My friends indicate that I am somewhere in stage four, moving quickly into stage five!

The only wisdom I now claim is that I have continued doing for many years what I have always been doing. And it seems to work.

I am more determined than ever to persevere and strive to grow. I'll be stronger in will, even more determined to survive, to seek, to find, and not to yield. I'll work harder than I ever have. I won't give in, I won't give up. I shall be the best I can possibly be.

Adapted from *Born to Raise*
by Jerry Panas

Jerold Panas is founder of Jerold Panas, Linzy & Partners, one of the largest and most respected firms in the field of campaign services and financial resource development.

One of the nation's most popular speakers on fundraising at conferences and seminars, Jerry is regarded as one of the foremost spokesmen in the field. He is the author of six best-selling books